Journey to Creating Harmony Within

The Flame

In the flame I see light, I feel warmth, I know peace

The flame moves yet I sense stillness

The flame reaches, waves and rests, its alive

Yet in one breath it can be gone

As is life

Too much fuel in life the flame becomes a danger

Too little and it can be lost

Nurtured cared for, it will stay true to life

The flames soothes, calms and is a welcome sight

More so in the darkest of places

Yet still reassuring on a bright day

See this flame as your soul

Recognise it for what it is

.....you

Keep connected with your flame

Nurture it and all will be as it should be.

By *Cathy Ferguson*

This beautiful poem was written by my lovely friend Cathy.
It truly captures the essence of our being, of our soul. Life
is all about balance, the dark and the light the yin and the
yang, the love and fight for our flame, that's in our heart.
<3<3<3

Earth Star Chakra

This chakra is not based on the body, it's about 6-8 inch below the feet. This chakra is an extension of the root chakra expanding your energies deep into Mother Earth, giving you connection and grounding, which I'll explain a little more in the root chakra.

My intent with this book, is to give you an insight into your own healing system within you and all the tools that you already have, that are just buried inside you. To awaken the spirit and soul and to help you enhance your life, as it has done mine.

The inspiration to divide the chapters by chakra was to allow you to work on yourself from the base up. The Angels were very clear on the delivery of this book. Each chakra chapter gives you an insight into the chakra, a little about me and a meditation.

I wanted to share that you don't have to be a guru or have special gifts. It's all inside you waiting to be tapped into.

I'm just an ordinary person with an ordinary life, just like you. I have a family of two teenage boys and I have my own complementary healthcare clinic where I offer a range of therapies.

In discovering more about me, healing and intuition, I've been able to help many people that come to the clinic and friends.

The question you need to ask is, how much time are you prepared to invest in yourself?

I've been investing time in me for around 10 years now and I still continue to grow - it's a never ending cycle of growth.

It becomes away of life, meditating, just being and letting things go, although somethings take longer to let go of than others and that's just being human.

I had always wanted to be a medium and I was truly under the impression that you actually have a conversation with spirit or angels and that you relayed what you've been told, which is not what happens as you will discover. However, I realised I had already been communicating with spirit, Angels and the universe and now my communications grow and so can yours. My journey revealed so much more than I anticipated.

What I realised is that our learning is individual, there is no set way to do something, apart from what works for you. Courses, workshops, reading are all ways to give you ideas in expanding your awareness and tools.

We are all on a journey, it's up to us how easy we want to make it. What lessons we need to learn or want to keep repeating.

I've discovered so much about me and really being the 'me' that I want to be. I understand how to have the universe work with me and not against me. It's when I get off track that I realise how much spirituality and the law of creation is a part of me and a part of this world.

I see life very differently now. I'm much more relaxed about life and understand when things are not to be, at that time. The world looks so different when you see things from another perspective and how much we can influence change around the globe starting with yourself. We don't realise the impact our energies have.

I wrote this book from my heart and with love with my only intent that it would spark something inside you and to see life through new eyes, the eyes of the heart.

My angels guided me along the way writing this book, which a big thanks goes to them for their input and their wisdom. Some parts I had to learn and experience before I wrote about them, which made me appreciate so much more about what I've shared with you in this book.

I was a big skeptic in all the spiritual side of life, thinking it was a lot of nonsense, little did I know that it was going to be a huge part of my life. I was worried and stressed all the time, frazzled trying to juggle life. Now I don't. I'm more laid back, stress free and think what will be will be.

I had my first reading when I was 21 and the information I was given was phenomenal. Accuracy of dates and times, how people passed over, descriptions of things blew my mind. At that reading, she told me how my life would change when I was 27/28 and boy was she right. Since that experience, that's when my curiosity grew and brought me to where I am today.

I had other readings from other people but I never got much from them not like my first reading, which has stuck with me due to the accuracy and detail.

As I mention throughout this book, please take from it what resonates within you. We are all different and what works for some might not for others. I've used what I did, what I felt worked for me and things I've tried but maybe didn't work for me. Keep your mind open to possibilities.

As you journey, you will come across more and more like-minded people that resonate with you. Friends will come and friends will go, such is life. When we understand the bigger picture we let go of fear and of judgement, we let go and we experience a peace that's so deep within us.

I've learned so much about love and self-love, we really

under estimate it and its power and how we use it.

I hope you get some inspiration from this book and that it will encourage positive changes in your life.

Root Chakra

For those of you who are new to the chakra system, the root chakra is the first chakra of the major seven chakras. Chakras are energy points that run up the centre of our bodies helping to keep us grounded and balanced. When these are out of balance, illnesses and unexplained emotions can occur.

This book is written about my spiritual journey relating to the chakra points. The root is associated to the beginning, the foundations, grounded-ness, survival instincts, vitality and strength and connection to the earth. The root chakra is based at the very bottom of your spine.

So with this in mind, it seemed a good place to start. So

we begin.

Like everything in life, there needs to be good foundations. Once you start on a spiritual and holistic journey, a good place to start is with balancing the chakras and balancing your energy. By doing so, you are giving yourself a good foundation to work from.

When you begin to open up to spirit, it's always a good idea to start the day by grounding yourself. By grounding yourself, you set yourself up for the day feeling calm and centred. This is a simple exercise to do in the morning time. Closing your eyes, taking three deep breaths right down to your abdomen and visualising roots coming out of your feet, down into the soil into mother earth, giving you a solid connection and strength is a good foundation to start the day. When you are not grounded, you may find that you have a spaced out kind of feeling and daydream a lot, which is ok to be in sometimes however if you are in this state too often, it's hard to differentiate between spirit and the ego.

Protection is the other visualisation to when you are grounding. The best way to do this is to imagine Archangel Michael's wings embracing you and to ask in your mind for Michael to protect you throughout the day and to keep you safe and protected in his wings. Archangel Michael is the protector and defends people. Michael means "who is like god". Some people like to imagine a blue light around them too.

These visualisations are to fix the intent of grounding and protecting - it's the fixing of the intent that's the most important. Intent is powerful and one of the spiritual laws.

When we balance the chakra energy it helps to provide clarity and in doing so, it allows the spiritual work and inner healing to begin. Having the chakras in balance is important but does not mean that they are cleared at this time as it can take a period of time to bring back the full harmony especially if emotions have built up over a period of time.

It is now putting this together that has made me realise how far I have come on my journey and what has been interesting is the synchronicities that are occurring, reminding me of my progress in teaching what I have learned and the importance of having good foundations - precisely what the root chakra is about.

My Journey Begins

How many of us really love ourselves, not in the egotistic way, but loving towards ourselves and grateful for the bodies we have. Honestly... not many of us, that's for sure and I was one of those people.

Once I opened up my heart and began to love myself for me a little more, the more I attracted love to me. Loving people was easy for me as I don't judge people and see the beauty in all. My learning was to begin to accept love and not push it away as I had done with family and friends, opening up spiritually is how I was able to do this.

Divorce is where my journey truly began. Oddly, divorce is what saved me and led me on a magical path of discovery, discovery of true love, discovery of spirit and the angels, discovery of the true me.

Looking back, I realise I already had a link to spiritual realms and the angels. My first memory being when my father passed away when I was sixteen years old. The week before my father died, my granny visited me (my dad's mum). She had died some 12 years previous but I could smell the sweet scent of roses and I heard her voice tell me not to worrying that everything will be alright. I remember feeling confused and thinking what exactly did she mean 'Everything would be alright'? Did I just imagine what just happened?! I forgot about the incident and never mentioned it to anyone for fear of being ridiculed.

Then the following week on February 16th 1996 at 03.15am, my father collapsed in the bathroom. He had suffered a massive heart attack and passed away. It was strange as I was very much aware of the energy in the house and I knew that he was no longer there - his essence and spirit had gone. The best way to describe it is when you come home from work and the house is empty. You can still feel the essence and spirit of those that live there - they don't need to physically be there to know they are safe and alive.

I could no longer feel the presence of my father and I knew he had passed away before we were officially told. The hardest part was getting used to the strange feeling he was no longer alive.

A month later I was in my room listening to music, - Robert Myles "Children" to be precise and clear as day, I could hear my father's voice talk through the music. I remember him saying that he was ok and was at peace. I don't remember what else he said as the shock of what had happened began to sink in. Thinking back, he was probably telling me to turn my music down! I tried to reset the music to the start of the track to see if it was on the music or if I really had heard my father's voice. Needless to say, I never heard the message again when I played it back.

I don't remember feeling fearful of what happened. I felt privileged that I was able to connect but shocked that it had actually happened to me. I wished too hard for it to happen again and it didn't until some years later.

As painful as my divorce was, I had the voice of my granny telling me everything would be alright again, which resonated with me as I knew in my heart it was the right thing to do. I later realised that the pain I had experienced wasn't for the loss of my husband (the then love of my life), but pain from the fear of change. For once, I had no control over my situation or destiny and this was the beginning of my learning to trust in the angels and the divine.

I kept hearing in my head 'This is for the best, the best is yet to come'. At that time, I couldn't see it. "Who would want me now?" kept playing over in my mind and it was a battle of the ego and the heart.

As the months rolled on, I slowly began to embrace the changes. My home had changed as well as my direction in life. I began to study Complementary Therapies at college, something I had always had an interest in and curiosity of. From the moment I began my studies, I knew I had finally found my life's purpose and it opened up a whole new journey for me, one I quite hadn't planned for.

Studying a full time course, working part time and looking after two children and a home was a tall order but somehow I managed it, along with the loving support of my mother.

As I have sat here and written about what I accomplished, it amazes me how I ever managed it. It's reflecting now that I realised I had the help and support of the angels guiding me through and I am so glad that they did. They wanted to push me on as I have a lot to offer and also help people, which, I now achieve through my Complementary Healthcare Practice.

One thing I wasn't prepared for when I began my journey in holistic therapies and healing, was looking at myself!! In order to help others, I needed to help myself. In doing so,

I hadn't realised how disconnected from life I was.

Up until then, life was just going through the motions but not actually feeling the *Emotions*! But once the power was restored to me, I began to experience true emotion and a connection to myself - I began to see my true self-worth.

Modalities like massage, reflexology and Indian head massage were good places to start and looked at the physical aspects of me and helped to bring my body and energy back into a kind of balance. They helped to reduce my stress levels, even though I hadn't felt stressed and I began to realise that I had been pushing my emotions down, rather than facing them and dealing with them, hence the disconnection.

I then began the reiki healing training and what a life changing event that was. I remember being told reiki finds you, you don't find it. I had previously been told by a lecturer at college that I should do reiki but at that point, I had no interest in it and I thought it was spooky stuff and a bit weird. However after reading an article at university a year later about a nurse that had used reiki during palliative care, it struck a chord deep inside me that I had to go and learn how to do it and then everything fell into place. A woman at university knew a reiki master who was willing to teach us and took us all through reiki training, up to master level. I recall my teacher saying 'Remember things will change and things will happen that will surprise you, but in time it will become confirmation'.

That very night on my way home, I heard a voice clear as day in my head telling me to come off the motorway a junction early. I remember having an argument in my head, wondering where the thought had come from and why I had followed the instruction. As I proceeded to come off the motorway a junction early, on the approach to the roundabout the news on the radio came on - the junction that I would have taken had been closed due to an overturned articulated lorry and I would have had a long diversion! The angels had definitely guided me that night and from then on, my curiosity grew I wanted to know more about the angels and spirituality.

So what is Spirituality?

At the start of my journey, I would have answered something along the lines as follows:

Spirituality is about connecting with beings that have passed, angels and being offered guidance in daily life by tuning into the unique energies of a higher vibration.

We are a soul and our spirit is the energy that surrounds us and nourishes our soul. It is the god's energy within us that is made up of many layers.

But I realised, Spirituality does not have a definitive answer as everyone is different and has a unique journey to follow.

That was then - now spirituality means so much more. Spirituality is you, the unique individuals that we all are. Being spiritual is becoming aware of you, away from the ego of the brain, working from the heart, connecting with our higher self and being completely in the now, where the past can no longer hurt us and the future is full of wonder and delight. There is no fear, only love. By being in the present moment, we instantly vibrate at a higher level and we are able to connect freely with the angels with clarity, as they are drawn to our love. Even when we begin the process of opening up, the angels know the love is there and waiting to come out in bloom to its fullest potential. By awakening the spirit within, you open up to accepting love in an unconditional capacity, love of everyone and most of all love of yourself. Every cell that creates the uniqueness that is you, with the love comes peace, joy and happiness - true happiness. True happiness comes from a state of being within, not from material possessions or the love of another.

In essence, spirituality is about unconditional love, where judgements and fear have no place to dominate our existence.

We become spiritual when we have found our true self, acceptance and bathe in the love of ourselves.

Take some time and ask yourself these questions, be completely honest with you answers as these are for you to evaluate where you are now on your life journey.

What does spirituality mean to you?
Do I have fears?
Do I recognise when to leave my fears behind?
What does love mean?
What is real love?
Have I experienced real love?
Do I judge people?
Do I hear voices in my head?
Do I follow my gut instinct?
How often has your gut instinct been correct?

So what are Angels?

Angels are heavenly beings that link our world with the spirit world. They work on the 5th plane of existence, the place of love and fear, good and bad, the plane that has high vibrational beings, gods and goddesses, angels, guardian angels, arch angels and our higher consciousness. We humans exist on the 3rd plane, a plane of illusion that creates reality.

Once you open up to working with the angels and your higher self, the messages that you get that you previously hadn't noticed are remarkable. How often has a white feather fallen at your feet or landed beside you? Have you never wondered why it's only white feathers!

Most birds that fly around my home or place of work are starlings, sparrows, magpies or crows (not many birds with white feathers) and why do they turn up in unexpected places and at times where you are looking for comfort and reassurance. I believe they are angels, letting us know they are there and can hear us.

There is a roundabout that I have to pass through on my way to and from work. Most times when I am at the roundabout, a white feather falls in front of the car but there are no birds flying about above for it to have fallen. It always makes me smile and feel grateful for all that I have in my life.

Angels are around us all the time and give us subtle messages like the feathers or music (when you turn the radio on at a specific song). These are just some of the ways they get your attention.

Anybody can work with the angels as they are only a thought away. Anytime you need help or encouragement, comfort or joy, then just ask them for some help. When you open up and accept the angels, it really is amazing what they can show you when you pay attention.

Ask the Angels simply by saying, Angels please help me with………………………, thank you or Angels please guide me to………………………. Thank you

A friend that was new to working and communicating with the angels had a magical moment when her daughters came in from being outside playing and found a rose pink heart shaped quartz crystal, out in the cul-de-sac near a field where very few people walk. The girls gave her the crystal and this was confirmation to her the angels had provided the answer to what she was looking for at that time. This strengthened her belief in the angels. She also shared her knowledge of the angels with her children and one of her daughters asked her if she could talk to them too, "Of course" she said, "Just ask Archangel Michael to come and look after you". As her daughter did so, she started to laugh and giggle as she could feel him tickle her ears, how amazing.

The angels are quite humorous too! Sometimes in our wee group, we can be in fits of laughter for no apparent reason! At the beginning of one meditation in particular, I remember bursting into fits of laughter. This had a knock on effect and all of us started to laugh - mainly laughing at me with my outburst - but it was good and it lightened the mood and reminded us all that we don't need to be serious all the time.

Beliefs are something that will crop up and this is something you need to ask yourself, 'What do I believe in?' You do not have to belong to a religious group to enable you to have beliefs, whether it be god, Buddha, Shiva, Allah, angels, the universe, the divine or whatever.

What I discovered is that god is not a person or being, but the god from within, the god that is you, god is love. Finding that god within allows for you to have beliefs of your own and most importantly the strength and the courage to believe in yourself! When you believe in yourself, miracles will happen.

God for me is source of energy, the deep love that's inside us all.

As I connected with my god within, I had the help of the angels guiding me, people, items and situations came into my life at the right time to help teach me and show me what I needed to know. These were not mere coincidences, these were orchestrated from the divine, teaching me to trust and believe.

Initially I struggled with believing in the angels as I felt silly and I would argue with myself. At our wee circle, I used to struggle with the meditations at first, it was because I thought I was getting something until I realised it was my ego wanting it to be which gave me the sense of being stupid, but as the weeks went on, I could not deny the fact that I was feeling energy and beings around me. Archangel Michael was one angel I felt. For me, he appears as a blue light with a strong sense of strength and protection. When my father is around me I get a smell of tobacco smoke and I can feel the energy of him of what he was like when he was alive. Also when he is around I see butterflies. When I moved home, I had a butterfly appear in the kitchen and then at the new house a butterfly appeared again. Two in the one day is quiet something as you don't see many of them about. Also, one of my spirit guides has a distinct smell of turmeric!

Now as my senses have grew I can see Archangel Michael as a flash of light particularly around someone who is needing to call upon him for strength and protection, or sometimes just to let me know he is there. After doing a meditation with my eldest son and we were talking about what he saw, he spoke of someone blue in colour and the name Michael. I knew instantly he was referring to Archangel Michael but I knew I had not mentioned him to my son. As I was telling my son about it being the Archangel Michael, a blue flash appeared at his head and he got a shiver run down his back. That was Michael letting him know it was definitely him.

What I have discovered is that there is no right way or wrong way to develop your senses. Everyone is unique. Some people see, some people sense, some people hear, some people smell, some people just have a knowing, some people get a mixture and that's ok. We were all born with the senses but lose them along the way as conditioning and social acceptability commence. Up until the age of around seven, our brains operate in the theta brain wave which is much slower and allows us to access much of subconscious mind, then it changes to the beta brainwave which is much faster and more of our conscious mind. This is another reason why much of what happens in our childhood can impact us in our adult life.

Finding a group of liked minded people is always a good idea. That way you can grow and learn from each other, even the teacher is always learning. With spirituality there is no end to the potential of growth. Once you learn so far you go back to the beginning again and you start over. This time you will be learning on a deeper level, then go back and keep going back and the depth to your knowledge will keep growing.

What is remarkable is when you are in a group like our wee spiritual group, when you meditate together and you link in with each other and you get the same messages or images and that is mind blowing. We can all see the same picture or message from different perspectives giving a complete image often filling the missing parts for each other.

One of our recent meditations we all got bliss, we all felt bliss and we had the feeling of bliss for a number of days after the meditation. This was a reminder to us of how far we had actually came in our meditations and excited us all as what else were we then going to uncover.

Meditation is a good practice in helping the chakras and balancing your energy. Meditation is not as out there as you may think, where you have to sit crossed legged and chant OM all the time. Meditation simply means quietening the mind. Switching off the inner dialogue that often fills our minds and causes self-esteem and confidence issues.

By taking time daily even five minutes, it can have a huge impact on your life having true peace and quiet for yourself.

Take five minutes just now, read though the steps first then have a practice:
- Close your eyes
- Focus on the breath, breathing in deeply filling your lungs and abdomen and   hold for a minute
- Let it go, out through your mouth
- Repeat the deep breath in and out through your mouth
          keep the focus on your breath
- Let any thoughts drift in, don't think about them, let them drift out the same way they drifted in
- Continue to sit like this until you feel ready to return to the room
- You may get messages, images, colours that's ok

Well how did you find this? It's not as easy as it looks! Probably the first time you tried it and only managed a few minutes. Keep practicing and you will be able to continue longer.

Initially five minutes can seem like a lifetime! You will soon realise the benefits and the impact this can have on you.

It's a good idea to have a journal to record what happens during your meditation. Now the basics of meditation are covered, looking back at balancing the chakras we can use meditation to focus on areas. As we go through this book, there will be meditations to look at each chakra in turn there will be other meditations to help also.

Meditation helps you to access the deeper subconscious of our minds. There really is a whole new world in there for you to discover. We only use around 20% of our brain in our waking life and that leaves 80% of your brain that can be accessed particularly the akashic records, where all the imprints of all our lives are said to be stored.

When I first began meditating, I found it difficult to do unless it was a guided meditation. My meditations began after setting up our wee spiritual development group in my clinic. It had three members and now almost three years on we have a solid group of five very strong and powerful women.

Initially for me, the meditations kept providing me with symbols which over time, kept recurring and I had to depict what they meant to me. There would be hearts, butterflies, pyramids and stars either five pointed or eight pointed stars. I'm not going to go into what these symbols mean here as what I discovered was that no matter how much I tried to understand what they meant through interpretations, it actually had a meaning that was more unique to me. When you uncover the meaning it will be a lightbulb moment.

So what I am saying is listen to your own inner dialogue and find the meaning that resonates with you, not someone else's, be open to the fact that sometimes the symbol has more than one meaning depending on the situation.

My hearts and butterflies for me were to do with self-love, the fact that I needed to find the love in myself to open up to change the inner me. I kept getting these symbols for weeks, months even a year until I finally listen and accepted what I was getting and making the journey to find me.

Meditation is a good way to find guidance from the heart, the true you.

Below is a meditation for the root chakra, either have someone read the meditation to you or record it and play it back. It's important to take your time and have pauses during the meditation to gain the full benefit. Allow the feelings, emotions and thoughts to come up to clear.

Root Chakra Mediation

Close your eyes, take a nice long deep breath in, hold and exhale.

Take another deep breath in and feel all the muscles of your body relaxing muscle by muscle, as you exhale let go of all the stresses, worries or cares of the day.

Feel the heaviness of your eyes as they relax, relaxing so much that it's impossible to open at this time.

In your mind's eye, imagine the sun above your head, bright and bold. Feel the warmth of the sun on your head. Take the warmth and pull it down through your body, relaxing the muscles as you do, lingering in any areas that you feel any tightness or tension. Let the warmth penetrate deep into the muscle releasing the fears and anxieties that reside there. Feel your body as it melts into the chair that you are sitting on.

Let the warmth of the sun travel down your legs like a gentle river flowing into all the necessary areas. Feel this flow go into mother earth like the roots of a tree, strengthening your being and your soul allowing your body and mind to be in perfect balance. As the beats of mother earth resonate through your existence you bask in this energy.

Take a few minutes and enjoy all that life has to offer, enjoy the beauty of mother earth.

As the magic of mother earth embraces you, nourishes your soul and replenishes your body, allow your body to go deeper, deeper towards the core of mother earth. Feel the heat and power of the magma, as this washes over you it restores you. Let the energy blend with you and become you absorbing the qualities and properties of mother earth. Feel the connection to mother earth and the abundance of life force that connects your root chakra to mother earth and all that she has. Feel as one with the universe, feel complete and whole.

Take a few minutes to truly absorb this amazing energy, which now you have connected with can reconnect with at any time.

It's now time to journey back, bringing with you, the energy you have found in mother earth. Your view of mother earth and her uniqueness has changed, your view on life has new meaning of beauty and simplicity.

Begin to feel the room in which you sit and the chair you are on. Feel your toes and fingers, feel the awareness return to your body. When you are ready, open your eyes.

Wow, what a powerful meditation! Your mind will feel so clear and a new sense of clarity and perspective. We often neglect the beauty the power and significance of mother earth and what she has to offer. We don't pay her as much attention as we should and our world is constantly harming her. As you become more aware pay attention to how she behaves, are the earthquakes that happen and tsunamis that have occurred really a big surprise?! Could it be her way of bringing people back together and our sense of community spirit that has been lost? Is it away of clearing the land getting rid of the old and preparing for the new? Could it be karma being repaid to areas that have really hurt and damaged her, food for thought!!

Being grounded on your journey is important as it helps to keep you focused and provide clarity into your insights. It helps to keep you balanced between spirit and reality, keeping us in the now and the present moment.

Signs when we need grounded are when we begin to daydream, feeling dizzy for no apparent reason, even arguing and not getting your point across, when you recognise any of these then redo the mediation or the visualisation earlier to ground you back to earth.

Tools to help on your journey

Crystals are another tool that you can use to help on your spiritual journey. Crystals linked to the root chakra are ruby, garnet, bloodstone, diamond and hematite. Meditating with crystals can also be beneficial as they can take you on a fascinating journey and tell you a story.

Carry the crystals with you and feel the qualities of the stone calm and ground you. These crystals are just suggestions relating to the chakra. What I find when choosing a crystal to work with, go with the crystal you are drawn to as there will be a reason as to why it resonates with you.

A year or two ago, I was at a local body and soul event where local traders of crystals, psychics, mediums and other new age people come together for the occasion. One such time I attended one with my youngest son, he had some money and was dying to spend it, so he had a look around and then when back to the stalls that had the crystals he was drawn to. At that particular time when we attended, he had been suffering from knee and lower back issues after falling from his bike and he was receiving physiotherapy for it. Anyway, all the crystals he picked that day were to do with spinal realignment. I was gobsmacked when I got home and checked them out, red jasper was his favourite and is known as the worry bead which was relevant to him at that time. It also cleanses the blood and the circulatory system which he would have needed to help the damage he had done to the area. The other crystal I remember he bought a few pieces of was selenite, which is good for the calming of the mind and realigning the spinal column and strengthening the skeletal system, which amazed me. He was a young boy of nine years and he had tapped into his intuition and the subtle energies of the crystals and selected the ones that would heal his body.

I do know that after using them he felt much better, the pain subsided quiet substantially and only required a few more sessions of physiotherapy. It's amazing what happens when we follow our instincts and trust!

Automatic writing is another tool in connecting with spirit, your higher self and the angels. I like to do this and it's outstanding the messages that come through. Parts of this book have happened this way. Initially similar to meditation, it's good to quieten the mind and just write the thoughts, words, and phrases that come in. It's when you read it back and you see you have a perfectly formed conversation and paragraph in front of you, that you don't recall writing! That's freaky but rather cool. You may also find that the writing isn't yours that's a strange thing to see. Sometimes I have seen my writing change a few times and this to me is indication that there has been more than one angel or spirit working with me.

Here is the first automatic message I received

"Blessed is the light that shines you on your way, be guided. Trust! Believe this is the key. Follow the wind be free, wherever it takes you be free!"

As you practice it, you might ask a question then wait for the answer. I have seen sometimes when I have written a reply to a text message and spirit or the angels have taken over and I read it back, there's no errors and has perfect flow. Normally I have fingers and thumbs when typing and make up random words, the curse of predictive text on mobile phones.

Parts of this book came flooding in this way, sometimes when I wasn't ready and mid treatment with someone - not the perfect timing - and I had to mentally ask for them to wait until I was able to write things down or provide me with a mental dictator phone. The number of notebooks I required was unbelievable, random bits of paper with writing on it took over. Even when typing on the computer sometimes my fingers just took over.

Dowsing is another means of asking yes no questions and receiving answers. Using a pendulum you hold it steady in your fingers and you ask it for a yes and for a no. For me a yes will rotate round in circles and no will rock backwards and forwards. Firstly, I will start by using obvious yes and no questions like is my name Heather "yes" am I 65 years old "no" (thankfully) although sometimes I feel it, but you get my drift of the context. After that, I will ask other questions I am looking for answers to in my life. I even use it at the start of the day to see what clients will turn up and which won't, usually it is correct. Sometimes if I ask it if a client will turn up and I get a no but it's only slightly moving, it normally means that no they won't turn up at 2pm, more likely 2.15pm. It's useful to give me an idea how my day is going to go.

Tarot cards and oracle cards are good tools to use. You

don't need to read them professionally, you can use them for yourself and I do have to confess here that I love using the cards. I have quite a collection of cards. I find I am drawn to a certain packs for different occasions, sometimes I use two or three packs. Initially, I found I did the cards first and read them, interpreted them and incorporated the meanings into my day. Now I find that I use them as a backup. For example, if I had done a reiki and gave some feedback from what came out during the session, always when I used the cards it just echoed what I had said, which was brilliant confirmation not only, for me but to clients too.

One recently that was remarkable, was prior to the reiki session starting, my friend was telling me that in the morning she heard a really loud noise almost like a bumble bee humming in her ear. She had asked her husband "Can you hear that?", to which he replied "No". Instantly, when she said what she heard I had the thought that it was her tuning into the frequencies of spirit. Already I had picked up the fact that the angels were there waiting for her to connect and ask them for help. After the reiki I gave her cards to pick and she selected three. The first one had the words presence and acceptance on it. The picture, I kid you not was of a little girl looking in wonder and a bright bumble bee that radiated light – how uncanny was that? That was precisely the image she had described, the little girl on the card was her. Confirmation that what we had discussed was right.

All these are just some of the ways that you can help to open up and connect with your spiritual side. What is important is that you do what resonates with you and that you feel comfortable with, but also practice practice practice….

Here are some essential oils that can help whilst working on the root chakra these include

- Sandalwood
- Cinnamon
- Myrrh
- Ylang ylang

These can be blended in a massage carrier oil and applied to the body or can be used in an oil diffuser.

Crystals for the Root Chakra

- Garnet
- Ruby
- Aragonite
- Red jasper
- Black tourmaline
- Chrysocolla

Message from the angels

Once our inner love for ourselves is found, it creates a strength and a power within. Confidence grows and your body and mind ooze vitality.

When we let go of all the pain and emotions that we choose to carry, our body energy flows freely without blocks. When we let it go our health returns.

The hardest part to understand and accept is when you are on your spiritual path that you have caused your own pains and own health issues and they could have been avoided, if we knew then what we know now. You don't consciously choose to be in pain but you do chose to hold on to the emotions that keep you stuck in the past. Chose to let them go, choose to be free.

Sacral Chakra

This chakra is found near the base of the spine and just below the naval, the lower part of the abdomen. The colour connected to this chakra is orange. This chakra is connected to sexual energy, emotions, relationships, abundance, wellbeing and healing.

When imbalances occur here, it can cause problems with our sexual energy and how we feel about sex, how we feel about ourselves and how we think and feel about our financial position.

As we get older, the sacral chakra can become blocked, more so for women. The reason I say this as women have more things to adapt and change to that can alter their perception of themselves through marriage and becoming a mother and they often lose sight of who they are. It does also happen to men too what I am saying is that it is more noticeable in women.

My experience happened when I got divorced and I had a real battle with my identity. I was no longer Heather Rankine, wife and mother, but neither was I Heather McCabe, who I was before, being a wife and mother and as my life had changed so much, now I was just Heather. Not that that was a bad thing however I just had to find out who Heather was again out with being Shaun and Callan's mum and the ex-wife!

This was when it dawned on me that I had really lost me! My self-worth and my true self. I had become absorbed in marriage and trying to be a good wife (which didn't do me any good!) and being a good mother to my boys and I trundled along in life forgetting all about myself, no wonder I had felt so disconnected!

As I opened up spiritually and accepted who I was, I began to reconnect to who Heather was and is and now after a long process I love who I am, a feeling I had never had before. Our wee spiritual group and using meditation and the going within that allowed for that to happen.

My orchestrated divine moment began during our weekly

meditations, as they began to centre on love, the feelings and sensations of what love is - was becoming intense. It made me feel anxious in a good way, as if I wanted it to hurry up. I was going away on a trip to Inverness on holiday to visit family and a long lost friend and I had the thought that I would meet someone when I was away. A few days before I left, I started talking to a guy and we got on really well and a few days after I got back, we met up for dinner and had a really lovely evening and agreed to meet again. I had a mixture of emotions running through me, but at the same time I knew something inside me was different. I was different and my perceptions of a lover/partner or soul mate had changed. I had allowed my heart to open up and for me to allow myself to love, me, a little bit more. By doing so I had attracted someone into my life and I was surprised by the emotions that it stirred up inside me, like was I ready for this but was this really what I wanted?

As I started to date the guy a book called "Loveability" by Robert Holden managed to find its way into my life. The book was amazing, it was like Robert had written the book especially for me and it taught me so much about myself. I started to do the exercises telling myself whilst looking in the mirror that "I loved myself".

This was very strange and very surreal doing these exercises. I remember going through a range of emotions doing this. At first I found it really difficult to look at myself in the mirror and utter these words to myself it felt very alien at first and then after a few times, I adjusted and it was ok and kept doing it. It is amazing how your body responds to simple caring words, it's like every cell of your body responds and your mood, your energy completely shifts, I was very impressed. It made me realise how far I had come to even consider doing the exercise and to even carry it out and it taught me how far I still have to go, but equally how far I had come on my journey.

A bolt of lightning hit me during my time dating the guy that he actually saw me for me the unique individual that I am. He hadn't judged me and the only person judging me was myself. I felt a wave of gratitude for this and I had to tell him. Before I would have held right back and worried about the reaction, but I didn't. It felt too important not to thank him.

My gratitude to him came from my heart and I felt safe and connected enough to be able to express this to him and my message was delivered to him with an open heart.

The gratitude had raised my kundalini energy and my sensual side began to rise. This wasn't about "sex", this was a connection on a much deeper level. The feelings I had, had sparked something inside me and made me feel more connected to my feminine energy, I felt whole and womanly.

Even on a sexual level I am more comfortable and sex is no longer the mechanical mechanism that it is thought of in western ideas, it is so much more!

Never before had I thought or explored the fact that touch and the use of your breath can create heightened sexual sensations, awakening your body bring about a mind body experience.

Loving yourself – truly loving yourself down to each wrinkle and cellulite on your thigh, the extra lb's of weight you carry, having that deep unconditional love for yourself and others and connection of oneness is what really heightens your sexual experience. Understanding that brought new spiritual growth and completed the part of the jigsaw for me. This connection and sexual and sensual pleasure was what I had thought an intimate encounter should be like.

Although the relationship didn't last longer than a few months, that was ok. It showed me that it was alright to be myself and express myself on many levels, although at times I felt vulnerable expressing myself on a deeper emotional level in a whole new way. I know that I spoke from my heart and I felt comfortable knowing that I had shared my feelings honestly.

I know that partly the relationship hadn't worked as I had stepped into my power and I was comfortable with who I was (am). What began to happen was it was highlighting to him that he was lost, he had lost is identity and by focusing on wanting to "fix me" by him feeling needed by me took the attention off of him and his disconnection to his life. He wasn't ready to face his issues so he went on his own journey.

I am grateful for what the relationship showed me and how far I had come in being Heather again. No way would I bow to someone else again. I had an inner strength and independence that made me ME. I knew this was a trial run and that I will be with someone that connects with me spiritually and allows me to be me and that's what we all deserve.

The journeys end with this guy taught me that although he allowed me to reconnect with my feminine energies, which I don't need to have the physical connection of another. By being comfortable with yourself and exploring yourself and your sexual desires, you can keep your femininity alive. It doesn't have to be lost. If you don't know who you are sexually and what creates the power to ignite you, how can you connect with another expecting them to achieve it for you?!

So what is kundalini

There is lots written about kundalini and a number of definitions of what it actually is. The definition that resonates with me is that kundalini is a heightened energy that lies dormant at the base of the spine and becomes activated through esoteric and spiritual connections, where we connect with our own enlightenment and experience bliss, true bliss. Although it lies at the bottom of the spine, it connects up to the sacral chakra and it's believed that the energy flows in a triangular way, flooding the pelvic area. When you harness the power and energy through kundalini awakening, you can train the energy to flow through your whole body, pulling it up through each of the chakras, intensifying your spiritual awakening.

Kundalini yoga is one way that this can be achieved using a systematic approach.

My awakening began through the meditations and my gratitude that this guy had taught me. It was the first awareness of the power of gratitude and the positive effects it has on the body.

As the gratitude filled my head, the angels were with me as I sat in my treatment room, being bombarded with the bones of this book, you hold in your hands. Birthing the idea of a spiritual journey that had taught me how to love myself on a deeper and more complex level than ever before and how the awakened feminine energies allowed me to connect with this guy, in a way I had never experienced before. Being honest and open from the heart. How touch, soft touch can be so electric and orgasmic than sex itself.

That sex itself is underrated, when two souls connect their touch, their synchronicities of their breath heighten their pleasure and that it is felt through every cell of their bodies and their bonds deepen.

By connecting with yourself and being true to yourself, love fills all of your body.

As kundalini begins to awaken there are usually pre awakening symptoms as you could say. These include:-

- Changes in the mind and thought processes

- Visions

- Vivid dreams that appear real

- Insights

- Synchronistic events

- Seeing the world differently

- Changes in perspective, how you think and perceive things

- Eyes opening wide as the mind quietens and absorbs

As you advance and spiritual awakening begins to happen you may experience the following:-

(*These are just guides and my experiences*)

- Sudden rise of energy and sense of energy

- See nature different, seeing the beauty in nature that surrounds us and the vivid colours it has to offer

- Sensations of time standing still, losing the sense of time altogether

- Experience healing symptoms, rushes of energy and flashes of light, blue, green, yellow
- Information being "downloaded" to you
- Receiving information about your life purpose
- Revelations of past lives coming back, giving a deeper understanding to you

Once we begin on a spiritual path it is hard to turn back. Our minds are open and expanded and life is completely different. Sexual energy is important when raising the kundalini and enhancing our spiritual flow.

Kundalini is achieved by a perfect balance of feminine and masculine energies existing in the body at the same time.

Tantra and Sexual Energy

I feel here I need to touch on tantric sex as sexuality is linked to the sacral chakra and is an important part of life. Tantra means "woven together", the joining together of energies. It's important to note that it is not a philosophical or religious however it is a technique to learn, pleasuring right to the soul.

I was in my early twenties when I read about tantric sex and I was impressed by what I read, but at the same time, it sounded familiar. Natural - the way I had expected a loving relationship to be. My husband at the time wasn't interested as it was "weird" for him.

It wasn't until years later when I revisited the tantric aspects of sex. Like I mentioned earlier to me this was how sex should be when you connect with yourself and partner. The real orgasmic part is the connection that's made through touch and exploration of each other, of the scents of each other, the taste of each other, the anticipation of each other all heightens the pleasure effect, the union of two souls connecting. Where sex is not perceived as sinful but sacred and divine, where goal setting is not required just the connection of two souls entwining, releasing the sexual energy that rushes throughout your body.

Honouring your body is paramount and having confidence in yourself with what you like and don't like sexually, comes with the trust you have in your partner. Having a tantric sexual experience increases your connection and bond with each other. As the energies blend you become more aware of each other and spiritual experiences can begin through these heightened energies that emanate. The spiritual happenings occurs as the souls unite triggering a blissful state allowing you to reach more directly to your higher consciousness.

I'm not saying sex in general makes you spiritual no! But experience sex in a tantric way yes, by allowing all your senses to come into play. Sexual pleasure and orgasms are much much more pleasing and tingle and penetrate every cell of your body and mind when you connect to each other on a deep level.

Sex is not something that can happen where "no strings are attached"...it's physically impossible. Energies from both parties blend creating and energetic bond maybe not consciously but subconsciously. This applies to general sex as well as tantric, as energies still blend and touch each other on different levels connecting you in a heart or soul way or both. So if you find yourself in a predicament where you are offered sex "with no strings attached", think twice as bonds will form and someone always gets emotionally hurt.

Sex and love through tantra go together, as sexual connection comes through the heart not the mind. The Kama Sutra deals directly with sex and love (Kama meaning sex and love) and that they go intrinsically together, they're undivided and indivisible inseparable creating a wholly union with you and your partner and the universal energy of all that is.

Although with our partnerships we can have a tantric experience without realising it. When we understand the concepts of tantra it can take your pleasures even further when we are consciously aware. It transports you into a place of being, rather than doing, raising your consciousness. Making love opens up to a gateway of sexual and spiritual energy and awakens the power within.

The key point's for tantra are being in the now and breathing! Yes a good idea to breathe but breathe deeply, breathe right down in to your abdomen and feel the breath fill your whole body, similar to what you would do in meditation. This gives you an awareness of your body and helps to keep the mind clear.

Next relax! Easier said than done when you are pleasuring your partner, but remember the more relaxed you are the more you will feel. Go with the flow and what you are comfortable with. Release yourself from the fear and go with your feelings. Unleash the wild side of you and let go. Feel with your body allow all your cells to rush with sexual energy invigorating you and heightening your senses.

Then, keep eye contact! This isn't always easy most people have their eyes closed during sex and let their minds wander and fantasise of their famous idol, well not now, keep eye contact and keep your souls connected to each other. When our eyes connect our souls communicate on a level that words cannot reach. We see the deep truth in our lovers and let go of our vulnerability, we open up to each other that wouldn't be achieved verbally. The eyes truly are the window of the soul, allow your partner to connect with you on the most sacred level of your being.

Making sounds, by that I mean sounds that elevate your pleasure and enjoyment. Why, you might say? Well, sound is an energy and helps to move the energy round and raise the vibration and helps heighten the pleasure mechanism, let your roar be heard!

These are really simple basics to help you get started. Touch I cannot emphasis enough the importance of as this is what builds the anticipation using gentle strokes smoothing the skin, avoid going straight to genitals, this should be last. Explore every part of each other's bodies all the grooves, scars, blemishes, contours of each other. Honour and respect each other's bodies, all the blemishes that make each us unique. Our bodies are the temples of the divine within each and every one of us.

Allow the blending of each other's energies to begin!

Feel each other's bodies, stroking down the arms, light brush strokes down the back of the spine, griping more at the thigh then as your hand gently rubs and caresses the inside of the thighs, kissing softly in the meantime, being aware of the softness and tenderness of the lips and the light kisses. Kiss down the body, kiss down the mid line between the breasts and gently skimming the surface of the nipples and down the side of the breasts. For women, this heightens your pleasure, often it can give you a heightened feeling and that's before the real work is done! Run your fingertips lightly down to the abdomen all the time breathing deeply and keeping eye contact, making sounds and staying relaxed. Feel the heat of each other and the tantalisation of each other's skin touching together. Your breath deepening with each touch. Taking your time, being gentle all the time keep movements slow, soft and delicate.

When it comes to touching the genitals, keep it soft and to a minimum. Sacred juices will be flowing and senses will be high. The heightened connection without the need for penetration can happen through touch alone, as you activate the sexual sensors within your body through the delicate touch and respect of each other.

When it's time for penetration keep it real slow. For males if they want to last longer, try riding the wave, taking things almost but not quite to the peak. For males abstaining from reaching their peak, this can be liberating as they harness the sexual energy within their bodies. This helps you last longer. Woman also can do the same giving you longer to reach the depths of each other through the energy exchange. Use the sexual energy to rush through your body energising and revitalising you.

Another tip for woman is use your pelvic floor muscles to massage him when he is inside you. Get the man just to insert it with no movement from him and you kiss tenderly as you are massaging. This helps create a bond and deepens trust between you. Tantric sex is a communication between the souls of each other, it should feel natural. It's almost a meditative state you both reach as the breath synchronises, bringing connection and togetherness. It's a state you both reach being in the now, in the absolute present where only love can be felt.

Don't worry if it doesn't all go to plan at the first time, that's ok. It's practice and adapt things to suit you touch, breathe, and stay in the now, eye contact, slow and gentle these are the basics and you won't go far wrong.

Women take control, unleash your femininity that is deep

within you its ok to connect with yourself, this radiates out an inner beauty, let go of the guilt an realise it's natural. Use the sexual energy to ripple through your whole body making you feel alive.

There are many articles and books out there about tantric practices and I suggest you have a look at them to expand your knowledge, what I have touched on is only a tiny minuscule piece of the wealth of information out there.

Enjoy your journey!

Although the tantra I have spoken about here is in relation to sexuality, tantra is a way of life. By following a tantra life it allows you to follow a bliss that opens up your heart and fills your life with freedom emotionally and enhances your health and vitality. Relationships become boundless and life as you know it is liberated and consciousness is expanded into the great universal flow. It opens your heart to unconditional love, a love of yourself. It does open up a vulnerable side to you also, as you are opening your soul to your souls mate.

Tantra is all about connection and the union that is bonded with two souls. The electric charge that is fueled between two bodies that ignite the passions within.

With tantra, loving the body, your body and your partner's body exploring and discovering new ways that tantalise the whole being to a new fulfilling level, connection with each other on levels no other can. Learning that sexual arousal isn't just about "doing the deed" but skin to skin contact, touch, synchronicity of the breath, becoming entwined in each other physically, mentally, spiritually and emotionally allowing each other to connect and be in the now, the present moment, where the past and the future have no purpose just the feeling of connection and blending of souls.

Tantra allows us to be free from judgement and ego. Tantra allows us to be free mind body and spirit. This is why a tantric life is a way of life, it allows us to be free from the constraints of society and live in the bliss beauty and glory of our own divine self and that of others we choose to connect with.

Sexual energy is as important as breathing. This unique energy helps us to connect to ourselves helps to raise our vibration and helps fill us with vitality.

The power of touch reconnects us back to source. Touch allows us to feel who we really are. Touch allows emotions that are stuck to be freed. It allows the love to start to flow again and takes us back to our heart place. Touch nurtures our soul, touch allows the ego to be released and it allows our mind to be calmed.

You

It's not just our intimate relationships that matter but our relationships' with others. Friendships can come and go and it's realising that, that's ok - it's part of the process of our growth. Some people are meant to only be in your life for a short period of time to teach you something. Sometimes it's the part of the journey you have to go together, or maybe you have something to teach them.

Then you have the ones that are there for you all the time. Your journey is together teaching, learning, supporting, loving and guiding you all the way. The ones that encourage your growth.

People we meet, come to us through the matching of energies at that time, or the thoughts they have put out there, meet what they or you require at that time. How often has your path crossed with someone at a time that was crucial to you?

A woman who I met and now regard as a friend, our paths collided when our sons became good friends, around a time that she was preparing to have surgery. A simple offering of reiki to help her through her operation, opened up a whole new chapter in both our lives. I came into her life at a time where, spiritually things were taking off for her and she was lost and struggling how to deal with it all.

My offering of reiki opened her up spirituality and I was able to offer guidance through her experiences and help her heal from her surgery. It had taught me how far I had come on my spiritual path and provided me with an opportunity to teach, but also teach me by taking me back to the beginning and experiencing it all again, with a fresh and deeper perspective.

By a simple gesture, I opened up a whole new lease of life and chapter in my friend's life. I helped her regain balance in her life, boost her confidence in all aspects of her life and let her realise her true self-worth and most of all to trust, trust in herself.

Then there are the friendships that were born through our wee spiritual group with Lorraine, Cathy, Anne and Jane and we have a strong connection of sisters, our sisterhood. We helped each other to mould and grow spiritually and as individuals, our spiritual family who without them I would not have developed the way I have and be where I am today.

I am lucky to have Kate my longest friend and someone who will be in my life until the end. She has been the one that's been there and listened to me when I have been at my lowest and someone who I can always turn to. She is non-judging and supportive and means the world to me.

I am fortunate to have my friend Luciana back in my life, who without the help of the angels I might never have found again. Luciana and I met through school and through a series of circumstances and her moving 200 miles away we lost touch. Then one day after searching for years I asked the angels to help guide me to her. Now she is back in my life and will never be leaving again.

And finally I have Jackie, who I met as I began my journey

of discovery, someone who supports me and nudges me out my comfort zone, helping my personal growth and teaches me.

I am so unbelievably privileged and grateful to have such amazing friends in my life and I hope I am as a good a friend too them as they are to me.

I now have a newfound peace inside me that, intimately I am comfortable with who I am and me as a whole, I am happy I have found Heather!

Knowing yourself is empowering!

Above all, the relationship that is the most important is the relationship that you have with yourself, as ultimately,this impacts on how we act with others.

We recognise the relationship connection to this chakra and the importance of the relationship with yourself and knowing who you really are? What questions does this stir up inside you?

- Do you feel worthy?

- If not why don't you feel worthy?

- Do I respect others?

- Do I respect myself?

- Am I comfortable about my sexual desires?

- Do I feel empowered?

- Do I know my life purpose?

-   Do I get along with others?

These are just some of the questions to help you get started exploring more in depth to how connected to yourself you are. You may find other questions arise and that's alright; it's your journey of self-discovery and connection to source.

Once you have found your connection you realise that inevitably you are connected to all that is, earth, the universe the chair you are sitting on, everything you touch we are all one.

Read through the meditation below. Don't rush this meditation take your time, especially when the soul pieces are returning as this is your lifetimes worth.

Enjoy!

Sacral Chakra Meditation

Take a few deep breaths, close your eyes and focus on the breath as you inhale and exhale. Feel the breaths as they fill your body, relaxing every muscle and feel the tension release from your arms, your fingers, your legs, your toes, your head and your face.

Take another long deep breath in, hold for a few seconds and exhale, feel the tensions release as the stress and worries of the day melt away.

Use the heat of the sun above your head and guide the heat down your body, paying particular attention to the areas that feel tight. Feel as the heat softens and relaxes the muscles in that area.

Now take your awareness to you sacral chakra. See or feel an orange colour spinning. Is it spinning fast, slow or steady? Is it purely orange or are any other colours visible? Is the orange deep and intense or bright in colour?

Take yourself deep inside the spinning orange colour, really allow yourself to go deep inside and feel the orange wash over you and empower you.

Bathe in the orange colour for a few moments...

Ask in your mind's eye for your soul's particles to be returned to you purified for you to your highest good. Feel parts of you return that have previously felt as though they were missing. Fill your whole being, feel your whole body and mind become complete, one and whole.

Feel the cells of your body as they adjust to the completeness that is you. Connect to the energy of yourself worth, feel it fill your body - with this energy comes love and joy a feeling of serenity.

Sit for a few moments and enjoy the feeling wash over and through you, empowering you to your soul.

You have now unlocked the part of your subconscious mind that allows you to be true to yourself. Remember you can access and go back to this point at any time.

Focus again on the spinning orange colour at the sacral chakra. Feel the spinning as it slows and steadies. Shrink the orange energy back down to the size of a small ball not closing it, but enough to keep the energy flowing and in balance.

Allow the energy to draw in from the room back into your body.

Begin to feel your fingers and toes and the seat you're sitting in. When you are ready open your eyes.

That was quite a powerful meditation. Remember to make a note of your meditation in your journal detailing any images, feelings, emotions or memories it created.

Returning our soul particles is important and something I would encourage you do often. When we spend time with people, part of our soul dislodges and sticks to them, so it's only right that we request that part of us back - it is our divine right. It makes us whole again.

If you find that there are people in your life that emotionally drain you or you no longer have a desire to have an emotional attachment to them, the cutting of the chords exercise is a powerful to do. Then return to the soul particles meditation, just to complete the disconnection.

To cut chords, sit as if going into meditation, visualise in your mind's eye the person who you wish to cut chords with. Examples may be ex-boyfriends/girlfriends, or even mothers/father where maybe there is a lot friction or tensions between them. Although the parent will always be in your life, you can ease the difficulties by releasing the emotional attachments often this helps improve the relationship. This exercise is not solely to disconnect from another. Releasing the energetic chords, releases the dysfunction of the relationship and releasing fear and allowing love to harmonise our bodies.

As you sit and visualise the person, imagine a cord connecting you. Depending on the attachment between you, you may see string, rope, chord, chains or whatever and you keep visualising the chord being cut either with scissors, saw, axe, knife, chainsaw...until the connection is broken. I always ask for white or pink light or both to be sent to the other person and surround myself in pink light to heal the disconnection. The relief can be quite phenomenal and watch how the energy or situation changes.

Healing

We have been working so hard on this charka, these lower charkas are very physical and are connected to the physical aspects of our body and mind and our feelings. Often in our hectic lives we now have to work hard to heal our bodies and our minds, to help us to release the past so that it doesn't bog us down and hold us back.

When we can finally allow the healing to be begin, we get the flow back in our life. We get our creativity back and our juices flow for the passions we desire, whether it be art, music, writing, painting or whatever as long as it opens us up and allows our heart to sing and dance and take us into the joy of life.

When we are in this flow, of life our vibration is different. It's higher and faster we can feel happiness, peace and joy - it's harnessing this feeling to run through our bodies on a more continual basis that allows for you to live in a more spiritual way, free from the noise and chatter of your head, free from fear.

When we can heal our minds from the feelings and emotions of trauma or loss, we begin to heal the physical aspect too. Emotions play a vital part in our general health, negative feelings don't just lower our moods they impact our health. Nine times out of ten you can generally pinpoint an emotional trigger for all health conditions such as cancers, ME, fibromyalgia, diabetes and so much more. Illnesses are more connected to the emotions than the mechanical breakdown of the body and functions.

Healing begins as the body comes back into to a balanced state of homeostasis, finding a modality that suits you is important to help you achieve this.

Remember, also communicating with the right person can initiate healing as well. Just having someone offer some compassion and time and a chance to off load can be nurturing and healing.

We mentioned earlier in the root chakra about meditation. Meditation has astounding benefits to our general health and wellbeing, not just on our spiritual path, predominantly as it helps to counter the effects of stress which is a major issue for people in today's fast living society.

Meditation is great to learn as you can use this yourself in your own time anywhere. Sometimes initially to get started and to get into the way of meditating, is to go to classes to help you gain the confidence to do it on your own.

For me, during our group meetings, we enjoyed meditation. This gave me the confidence to do it on my own - even five minutes in the morning to start your day off has great benefits.

Reiki is another modality that works on the spiritual, the mental/emotional, physical aspects. It can help alleviate pain, help release blocked emotions that have become stuck and sometimes these may even be stuck from past lives. Clearing these blockages help the flow to return to the body providing a new lease of life.

Reflexology, massage, colonic hydrotherapy, chiropractic

care, acupuncture, shiatsu, osteopathy and yoga are all modalities that help move the energy in the body to regain equilibrium. Everybody is unique so find the one that suits you. The more you resonate and connect with the therapy the more you will gain from it.

Nutrition is one of the biggest things. We really are what we eat! If we are eating foods that have no nutritious value then his will impact on our health. Gluten is one of the biggest foods that we should avoid as the protein bonds found in gluten is difficult for our bodies to digest. It's added to so many foods to bulk out the food or sauce, plus it's the main ingredient in foods like bread, pasta and cereals which is in the west the major proportion of our diet, so is it any wonder that we have a nation that has a high demand on the healthcare services for bowel issues, mental health issues and heart disease? Children are increasingly becoming hyperactive due to gluten being introduced early into their diet, so reducing the gluten content in their diets and increasing fresh fruit and vegetables and meat proteins will alleviate these issues.

Without going on too much more into diet, as this is really another book in itself, gluten from a spiritual aspect will help clear your mind making your body and mind feel lighter and freer and allow you to be more intuitive with your body.

Healing is so important for our bodies, even when we are healed, it's always a good idea to keep the healing going as a form of maintenance as they saying goes "prevention is better than cure"

As you begin to heal you become more in tune with your body and how it works for you. You are more connected to the gut reactions your body gives off and you have more of a sense of who you are. When you eat something that doesn't work for you, you are more able to identify it. If situations don't feel right you are more easily able to hear your body tell you to get out of there.

One thing you do need is to practice is the art of listening. Listening to your body and listening from the heart! You will be amazed how much your life will flow more easily when you listen with your heart, even when you head doesn't agree, just trust in your higher self and your heart it will always guide you and keep you safe.

We do live in a world of kind hearted people. There are many open hearted ones around. Our media always portray the badness and sadness of the world, when there are so many random acts of kindness being done globally, how different life would be if we heard these stories daily?

Crystals to help you on your journey with this chakra include:

- Agate
- Quartz
- Calcite
- Garnet

- Carnelian

- Orange topaz

- Fluorite

- Diamond

Essential oils that can be used in massage carrier oil or diffuser are

- Jasmine

- Orange

- Mandarin

- Neroli

- Ylang ylang

Message from the angels

You are becoming the song of your heart. As the flower blossoms as do you, as beautiful as this is your connections to the earth taking root and pushing you forward, gaining strength and power. Enlightening you as you move towards your greatest power that is you! The light within shines out like a beacon drawing all the liked minded people towards you, with every breath you take you offer your life of your soul, your heart is open and in the flow, enjoy, enjoy enjoy!!! The joy of the universe is harmonising with you at this time. Enjoy and rejoice and sing with the angels on the rays of light and love, spread this high vibration spread the love and the joy, from the heart of the universe.

Embrace all that is you, the power and divine femininity that belongs within you………….. The journey continues, embrace into the infinity of love and life.

I

Solar Plexus Chakra

The solar plexus chakra sits between the naval and the sternum. The colour yellow is associated with this chakra point.

This chakra looks more in depth at you, your self-esteem, empowerment, gut instincts, and guilt.

How we feel about ourselves and relate to the outside world are critical. When this chakra is out of balance we are very judgemental of ourselves and others, addictions are common when this chakra is not in balance.

This chakra is our sun.   Just like the sun in the sky, it's the element of fire thus connecting our burning desires, it's our furnace of life and existence of our souls and is a power source of transformation.   Where our willpower is created and encourages us in our daily lives to step out of our comfort zone and push our boundaries, challenging us and allowing us to grow, your spark is the divine creation with in each of us.

Energy

Before we go any further let's discuss what energy is, well what energy means to me in terms of spirituality. We think of energy in terms of strength and vitality to power our bodies through the day and during times of physical and mental exertion.

But when we break it down further, we and all things on earth are made from energy. We are made up of millions of atoms that structure together to make human beings, or solid items like tables and chairs and they give off a vibration which allows us to feel energy!

When you become more sensitive or a light worker as some books refer too, you can feel and sense energy and change vibrations using emotions. Have you ever done the experiment where you rub your hands together really fast then hold them about an inch apart and pull them away until you can't feel the ball of energy between your hands? It is cool and gives you an idea of what it feels like. The more you practice, the more you are able to feel other energies.

What other energies do you mean? Well, angels and loved ones! Have you ever been upset and felt a presence around you making you feel safe, or feel a tickle on your face for no reason? I get this a lot when I meditate. That's when I know the children angels and cherubs are around being playful.

One time whilst doing reiki, I was working around the face on a client and I had a sense of urgency to clasp my hand round their jaw and cup their face in my hand as though a loved one would have done this to them, when they were alive. My hand felt glued to her face and I physically couldn't pull it off for a good five minutes. It felt like a loved one was so desperate to hold her again and assure her everything was okay and I saw roses being given so a lot of love was being given to her. At the end I fed back to her what I got and she felt it too. She felt as if someone had pushed my hand in to her cheek like her mother in law used to do and that was who she sensed around her.

Reiki is a good way to feel energy and sense what is happening in the body or in a person's auric field. You might sense pain, low energy, inflammation. Sometimes you can feel spirit around them. This is done by learning to feel the different vibrations of energy.

Once when I was doing my reiki training my reiki master had a friend of theirs come for a treatment so we could practice on someone we didn't know. We worked as a group and I was working at the chest area. What happened was incredible!! My hands were hovering just off of her body and working on the left side I had a sense that her left breast had been removed! I had no prior knowledge and certainly to look at her, you would not have known as my hands were hovering off the body, so I didn't physically feel it. I felt the energy and it was different from the right side. I also got the feeling imposed on to me that I myself had my breast removed just to confirm my findings. When I fed back my findings to the woman, she had confirmed that she had indeed had a mastectomy of the left breast!

Another time was working on someone that had arthritis and my hands looked like they were taking on the deformity the arthritis had caused, which was pretty freaky but once I moved my hands away, mine returned to normal.

Energy is all around us. It's what every object, human and animal is made up of. You don't have to do reiki to sense energy, being aware of energy helps you develop your awareness to situations and to life. How often have you stood in a queue and moved forward slightly because you felt uncomfortable about the person standing behind you? That's right you guessed it, they were impinging in your energy field and more than likely you sensed it didn't feel right as you hadn't invited them into your space!

So here is the challenge. Next time you are standing in a queue, try and sense what is going on behind you before you look and see.

Auras

We have spoken about energies and how we can feel and sense them. Auras are the energy field that surrounds us and is made up of a number of layers, which when we train ourselves, can be seen with the human eye!

The colours in the aura change second by second as a direct response to our thinking, our moods and our general health.

Recordings of auras date back hundreds of years, even with descriptions in the bible depicting halos around Jesus, Mary and many saints.

Cleansing of auras have taken place over the years too, with shamanic rituals and the use of smudging being the most popular and are still carried out today.

Your aura helps with gut instinct as your aura feels its way ahead of your physical body, alerting you to situations.

Here is a wee exercise that you can do to see the aura. Once you get the hang of it you will be looking at auras of people whilst standing in the supermarket queue.

Take a few minutes and quieten the mind, taking in a few deep breaths.

Have the person's whose aura you are reading sit by a plain wall, preferably white. As they are sitting look at their shoulder, then look just slightly past the shoulder. Relax your eyes almost in a sleepy gaze. Look as if you're searching past the person at the wall and you will see colours. It could be a block of colour at one side, it could flow in a colour round their body - you may also see more than one colour.

The colours do have meaning which can be looked at later, but the best thing to do is to practice as much as possible, getting the colours. Then once you feel more comfortable, ask the person to think different words as they sit, like love, war, death, toxins, hugs, kisses and sunsets and see how the colours around them change. You may also sense the energy of them like warmth, coldness, heaviness, lightness and so forth. As you practice, you may also begin to sense others around you like angels and spirit as you tune into the energy. For me, Angels sometimes appear as block of light with Archangel Michael being seen as a block of blue light. Often in our wee spiritual group, I have the colour yellow or orange pillars of light standing beside or behind me. Quite often between two of us in the group, we can both see the same colour.

I did this experiment with a group and one of the girl's

words was 'jealously'. I was standing beside her and I could feel the energy push me further from her, it also felt prickly and jaggy. The other girls that were there felt it too, they didn't have the repelling feeling I had, standing so close. Even though I have done this experiment a number of times, it was still a real eye opener as to how a feeling or emotion can affect your energy.

There is a great aura app that I had on my mobile phone. One day my friend and I took our wee puppies out for a walk. The pups were good friends too and they had had fun running about chasing each other. When we came home, I took a picture of our collie dog Hollie and what we saw was amazing! Beside Hollie was a matrix style image and you could make out clearly an energetic imprint image of Oskar my friends bulldog. The energy of him was still with Hollie. It taught me a lot about energy, just like the energy of Oskar was still with Hollie, the spirit of our loved ones is still there with us if we can tune ourselves into it.

Energy is your sixth sense and the more you practice using it and sensing it, the more aware and intuitive and sensitive you become. We were all born with this ability but lose it through years of judgement and conditioning as they creep in.

Understanding and reading energy should be an integral part of our life. If we can read energy from others, we would understand our friends, colleagues, humans and so much more. Animals communicate through energy. Why as humans, can't we?!!!

Here is another exercise you can try.

If you have a group of you, have someone blindfolded or sit with their eyes closed and with their back to the rest of the group. Have someone walk towards the person that has their back to everyone or is blindfolded and ask them to say 'Stop', when they feel someone in their energy. Then ask the person that's blindfolded to feedback to the group what they sense. Do they sense who it is? Do you sense any physical ailments of the person that's in their field? Do they sense or feel any emotions? Then have the person try and connect with the higher consciousness of the person in their energy field and ask for a message.

It will amaze you what you actually pick up. Try to take things further and see if you are sensing the energy at a soul level or auric level.

If you don't have anyone that you can practice with then you can use crystals, not that they will physically talk back to you, but you will be able to pick up on the energy vibrations that they give off. Rose quartz is a nice gentle crystal and has a nice calm loving energy. Clear quartz has a much faster energy vibration, where bigger pieces can be over whelming and can cause you to feel dizzy if it is too strong for you.

Once in a crystal shop, there was an abundance of clear quartz large and small pieces and I felt my whole body vibrate...quite an amazing experience.

Using crystals whilst meditating or whilst giving or receiving reiki or any holistic treatment, really adds to the benefits as the energies combine.

Energy when we think of it in terms of our body is our fuel, it's our driving force that gets us up and on the go and motivates us in life. The solar plexus is the energy fire starter. It's here that the spark is ignited to light your fire with your passions of creativity and zest for life. Physically it is here that the fire of our metabolism is ignited, the nourishment of the other lower chakras feed the fire giving us a circle of life. A flow of energy for our bodies to function physically, emotionally and spiritually.

Have you ever wonder how prayer and affirmations work? They come down to the power of words and the impact of the energy that they provide. Using positive words, providing positive outcomes, as the vibration echoes out into the universe you get your return as you add the feeling of what you desire, it shouts even louder into the universe. As Louise L Hay wrote, 'You can Heal Your Life!' How cool is that?!! All by changing one simple thought process from, negative to positive.

The energy of the words you say, pulse out to the universe and the universe delivers back the same energy vibration, therefore positivity will be delivered back with positive outcomes and negativity, well you guessed...brings more negativity.

This is often referred to as the law of attraction. Books like *The Secret* give good information on how the law of attraction works and how to use it your daily life.

Vision boards are another way of using the law of attraction, as you focus on the desires of your life and place it on the board, where you can see it daily. As you focus upon it, you draw it closer into your reality as your feelings intensify around it.

One of the tutors I had, told a great story of a car she was manifesting and described the make, model, colour and the private number plate, everything and then a few days later, low and behold she got a postcard through the door from a local dealership, with the car she wanted in the colour she wanted and the number plate! How cool! The only thing was that it was just a picture - a good lesson to be more accurate in what you want in life.

Get things clear in your mind and it will come to you. Don't dwell or wonder how it will happen, if you focus on your desire the universe will do the rest.

Think of a time where come hell or high water, you wanted something and you got it, then looking back you wonder how on earth that happened! You purely focused on the end result.

Energy is amazing when we know how to work with it, feel it and understand it.

Consciousness

We have spoken about consciousness but do we actually know what it means?

Consciousness simply means being aware, in the now. What our mind allows us to perceive and our insights we have about life. Normally there is something tangible that can describe the conscious awareness. When we are asleep or in a coma, we are not consciously aware of what is happening around us.

So what is the subconscious?

Sub consciousness is not something that cannot be seen by the eye, it's a knowing deep within the mind that can be accessed through the likes of meditation. It's a part of our mind where there is no judgement or reasoning it "just is". It can be described as our inner most thoughts and by tapping into them we can make them conscious in our daily life's.

So then what is God/Christ or higher consciousness?

This consciousness is when a mature level of emotional enlightenment has been reached, stability of emotions and living life in a joyful and loving way. This consciousness can be accessed through deep meditation, it feels light, a sense of purity and complete serenity. From a higher consciousness it's a part of you that you are able to reach, which contains the truth of our being, our purpose, our inner serenity and peace. This is the part that often "talks" to us, the part of us that we often ignore, then kick ourselves for not listening to what we already knew. It is here the ego battles with our higher consciousness our inner knowing. I have just read Kyle Gray's fabulous book *Angel Prayers* and describes the ego perfectly **E**dging **G**od **O**ut. This for me really allowed for me to understand this battle that goes on inside us daily. God is love and let that fill your consciousness. Dr Wayne Dyer also talks about this and its concepts in more detail, as we progress in life we become attached to possessions and people and it's this attachment that creates the ego and allows judgements to be created of ourselves and others.

The ego simply means "self" or "I", we are not born with an ego. As a child, we are born and discover others, our mothers, fathers, siblings we discover pure unconditional love, before we discover our self. We are born to only know, feel and give love. Through conditioning of life we discover our self, away from the connection of oneness, the all that is, the all that was at the time we were born. The ego can be a reflection of life a by-product of others thoughts, where in essence we have lost our self, if the ego is dominant.

The freedom we create for ourselves when we allow ourselves to truly let go of the judgements we hold against ourselves and others is liberating and empowering. Life flows to us rather than us going against the current of life. Stress and worry lift as we no longer feel the need or the desire to keep up with materialistic possessions, as we create a peace within us and an acceptance of the trueness of our soul.

The following meditation is to help balance the solar plexus letting go of the past and releasing our inner child.

Solar Plexus Meditation

Now close your eyes and get yourself into a comfortable position. Take a deep breath, filling all the lungs and abdomen, hold the breath for a second……. and release through the mouth. Take another deep breath in and hold, release through the mouth.
Continue to breathe deeply and slowly feel the muscles of your body relaxing, down your arms, down your torso, down into your legs.

Feel the energy burst out your toes and down into the energies of the earth below. Feel the energy as it begins to take root and connect with mother earth. Take the greatness of this energy and begin to bring it back up into your body, up your legs and into the solar plexus chakra through the base of your spine.

Feel this energy transpire into a deep intense yellow colour. Feel the intensity of the yellow colour flood the area, feel the intensity of the emotions or memories that is stirred up in this area. These may link to childhood, they may be uncomfortable, but just allow them to come up to be released knowing that you are in a safe environment to let the emotions go. Take a few moments to acknowledge these emotions or memories.

As the emotions now pass, feel the childhood memories of good times rush in and take over. Embrace the joy and the childlike wonder, the sweet and innocence of being a child again. Reconnect with your inner child, dance, play, laugh, sing with your inner child, and connect with the child within, embrace the freedom. Take a few moments to enjoy playing with your inner child.

Feel the energy of the yellow colour at the solar plexus chakra. Feel how much lighter it feels as the emotions connected there have cleared and your inner child has reconnected with you, bringing light-heartedness back into your physical being.

As we begin to journey back, thank your inner child for their connection. Feel the energy draw in from the room back into you. Feel the sensations back in your body in your arms and legs, wriggle your fingers and toes, when you are ready open your eyes.

You're back! How did that make you feel? Do you feel lighter and clearer?

Meditation can stir up old emotions that are ready to be dealt with. By dealing with them releasing them you make way for new feelings to come in and take their place, like anything though, change can be daunting and uncomfortable for a short period, but you come out the other side stronger and clearer and you will wonder why you never did it earlier.

One emotion that can come up that can be difficult is forgiveness. Sometimes we need to forgive ourselves. We are our own biggest critiques and judge ourselves harder than we would anyone else. We need to learn to be kinder to ourselves and do what is right for us not anyone else.

Forgiveness can also mean to forgive others. This can be difficult especially if it's something that someone has done to hurt you, for example if a murderer killed a member of your family, forgiving the person is not something that is easy to do, I understand. As you become more aware of yourself and how and why people behave in certain ways, you can forgive the person not necessarily the actions of the person. Even if the person has passed over you can still forgive, as it acts as a release of the past for you.

Holding grudges and resentments is bad for our health emotionally and physically. It's not easy to do granted but with time and a willingness to work on releasing, it makes all the difference.

Forgiveness allows the acceptance and frees you from the energy of the pain the person or situation caused. It allows you to regain your power. We have a tendency to get caught up in the past. Make this the turning point to let it go, it does not serve any purpose. Learn your lesson(s) and make peace with yourself. We only hurt ourselves by not letting go, the past can't be changed only learned from.

One thing I had to do was forgive my ex-husband and ex-friend for their part they played in my divorce. I am now thankful that I am away from the toxic relationships as the learning to forgive has opened up a whole new world and allowed for my life to move on in a way that I would not have done, had I still of been in the relationship and for that, I am truly grateful.

The most important person I had to forgive was myself! I hadn't done anything wrong. I blamed myself for being a failure, for not being a good enough wife, lover, mother and for the relationship ending. Opening up spiritually allowed for me to see the bigger picture of the situation and that powers higher than mine were unfolding and teaching me lessons, lessons of life.

Forgiveness allowed me to move on. I don't condone what happened but what I can say is that I am in a far better place in my life than I would have been if I was still married. I have achieved so much and most importantly found me. It pushed me out my comfort zone and made me look at life through different eyes.

Understanding ourselves and who we are is not an easy

task and takes surprise turns along the way. Frustration is one of them! As you get so far and are excited about the experiences of spiritual enlightenment you discover, and the synchronicity that appears and blows your mind, then suddenly it stops….. dead, nothing. You then begin to doubt your experiences does spirit and the angels, exist am I going mad, no is the answer. It's all normal to experience this, it's all part of the journey that you are on. The pauses often happen to allow integration of new knowledge and experiences settle in to you and allow the adjustments in your thinking and awareness in preparation for the next part of the journey. Then a jolt happens and propels you forward, it can feel familiar almost as if you have went back to the beginning again and you probably have but this time you will experience things differently and a deeper level of understanding will unfold. Spirit works by giving you little bite size pieces that you can deal with, as spirit knows what you are able to cope with.

I'm using the word spirit here as that's my understanding and preference, it may be the universe, higher consciousness or God to you, however ultimately they all relate to the same thing an unseen force that guides you. I intermittently refer to each one dependant on situations.

Remember everyone's journey is unique. Yes it's good to read other people's experiences to try and get a feel for how things are done, but most importantly do what you feel works for you - there is no right and no wrong way to do things. Some things you will read or experience that resonates and works for you and others won't and that's ok - trust yourself. Keep an open mind what might not work now might work later for you as you develop. Remember everything is in divine timing.

My mind is much more open to possibilities now than ever. Looking back I was quite regimented in my thoughts, my spiritual development has allowed me to grow as a person and a therapist. My therapies really embrace the whole mind body spirit element as my understanding and awareness is much more heightened than before. Trusting my intuition has allowed for me to help so many of my clients.

Spiritual development is not something that can be learned from books or workshops, it's a lifelong journey of constant discovery, exploring yourself and all of life, releasing old beliefs and patterns that have held you back in this life and past lives and future lives to come. It's a journey that starts from within. Workshops, seminars, books all give you options to explore however each and everyone's experience will ultimately be different. There is no right and no wrong, just being, just allowing.

We are a soul incarnated in a physical body, domineered by time of this reality. Our soul does not know time, only experience. As humans, we need to physically see us and the changes to occur for our mind in the conscious moment, to comprehend the here and now and understand evolution. Your soul knows where it has been and where it is going, your physical body is all that is required for certain parts of your journey and for lessons to be experienced and learned by you and by others, who are on their journey too.

I believe solar plexus issues arise with people battling with spirituality and the universal connection as they doubt and fear its existence. This is the last chakra associated with reality the physical part of our bodies, with the opening of the heart and connection to the spiritual realms. Often people that are opening up have issues of trust as it takes a complete leap of faith to trust completely and trust in the flow of life. It is here that balance between reality and spirituality is required. You don't want to be too rooted in reality and only see the black and white of life and equally be too spiritual and floaty that you have lost touch with reality!! As we are, after all, living in the human world.

Having the balance and being able to see life through all the colours of the rainbow and understand the difference between reality and spirituality. When we can merge the two worlds into our own we add much more depth, variety, love and acceptance into our lives that we lead here on earth.

Crystals of the solar plexus

- Citrine
- Amber
- Moonstone
- Peridot
- Malachite
- Yellow jasper

Essential oils for the solar plexus

- Black pepper
- Cedar wood
- Clove
- Cypress
- Geranium
- Ginger
- Lemongrass
- Rosemary
- Yang ylang

Message from the Angels

Forgiveness comes from within. Call upon your angels at any time to help with forgiveness as this brings a wave of freedom to your soul. Time is precious here on earth so don't waste it. Our energy is light, we have a warmth about us this will allow you to easily recognise our presence. Earth angels walk beside and among you all the time, if you refer to someone as an angel then the probably are. Be blessed to have connected with us in this way. Ask and we will assist as that is our purpose.

Heart Chakra

The heart chakra is all about love, joy and inner peace, located near the heart itself in the centre of the chest. The epicentre where mother earth our soul meets the universe of our spirit.

The colour connected to the heart chakra is green and can also be pink. The green is symbolic as it's the yellow for the soul merging with the blue of the spirit, creating green.

I personally had never made this connection about the heart chakra being the meeting point of the soul and the spirit and thinking about it, it makes sense. In order to open up, you have to have connections to the soul to understand you and a connection to spirit to what makes you... you!

When these are in balance and the awareness is there then the heart can fully open and expand and expel out the love to touch on everyone.

Our awareness is where we understand our true selves and it is here, we access our highest consciousness. As our previous chakras have taught us to stand in our power, we now trust in the flow of life, we have got out of the head away from logic and work from the heart, from love. There doesn't need to be an understanding of how things work, but accepting it just is. With *accepting* being the key word. Trusting in the universal laws of life, when you are in the flow of love and life the universe returns this back to you, as what you give out comes back, like attracts likes in many aspects of our life and this creates abundance. Abundance in love, opportunity, health, prosperity – everything.

So what is love?

Love is pure, unconditional love for all things including yourself, where there is no judgement and no fear, complete flow of life being completely in the now, the present connection to all that is.

As I write this, the Frankie goes to Hollywood song – *The Power of Love* echoes through my head, and the lyrics "Love is like an energy, rushing in rushing in inside of me". This sums up the power love has, it is an energy not an emotion, it vibrates out and touches everyone. When we are in the flow of love, the heart opens and we are in the flow of the universe.

Can you remember when you felt in love? Did anything matter? Did you worry about the past or the future? What made you feel love? What had changed that you began not to feel the love?

It might sound easy loving everything and yes sure enough it is easy to say you love everything but do you mean it? Do you believe it? Do you feel it?

No! I didn't think so.

But the big question is, do you love yourself?

You can't be in the flow of LOVE if you have missed yourself out as you are a part of the big picture of everything of the all that is. Pure unconditional love just like the unconditional love a mother has for their child, they love their child no matter what their flaws, or mistakes they have made, as they know that's how the child learns and unconditional love and support from the mother to the their child allows the lessons to be taught and allows the child to grow and blossom. The love is given back through the freedom of learning and growth.

Although not all parental love is easy and children can suffer abuse either emotionally, physically or sexually, this is another topic and where the parent has no self-love, respect or control. I want to acknowledge this as it is not the victims fault but issues of the parent and in both cases, forgiveness is required.

Love breaks away the barriers of judgement, it's when we are experiencing the NOW not the past and not the future expectations.

Can you image how it must feel to not know what love feels like? When I think of this question it makes me realise how lucky I am to have experienced love in and unconditional way through my parents, my children, my dog and my friends and I feel blessed that I can express love unconditionally.

How we get out of the flow of life?

The past is often where most of us get stuck, where past events prevent us from moving forward and grips us with fear, just like the experience of my divorce in the sacral chapter.

We get caught up in the analysing and the' What if this' and 'What if that'. But all said and done it can't be changed, we learn from it and move on and don't make the same mistakes again.

Death is the other common event that stops us moving forward. Death can tear us apart inside, but once we understand that death doesn't mean that the person has gone forever, they are gone to be reborn. Their spirit their energy will always be a part of you and always there. Death means that they have fulfilled their part that they have had to play on the earth plane for some it maybe years and for some not so many. When we understand that prior to being born they signed a divine contract mapping out our time here on earth, some people return to pay back karmic debt. The soul knows its purpose here.

Death teaches us lessons about ourselves and provides us with strength to carry on.

Once the spirit/soul passes they are not unhappy, they know that their pain or suffering has passed and know that they can be with loved ones all the time, helping and guiding us from the other side should we chose to open up and accept their help.

When my father died it was very hard. I felt cheated that he had gone and left me, sad that he never knew me as an adult of my life my achievements, angry that he never got to see his grandchildren that I know he would have loved. But now I have a peace inside me, a peace that knows he may not be here physically, but spiritually I now he is here watching and protecting me and my boys.

One such time I recall his presence was when we were involved in a car accident. My ex-husband and my eldest son and I were travelling home after trip from seeing my ex-father-in- law. We were travelling on a busy road in Scotland the A9, in the height of summer and the tourist season.

As we left my father-in-law's I had an unsettled feeling. Normally I would have fallen asleep on the six hour journey home but this time I was agitated, an uneasiness that something was wrong. We were two thirds of the way home and I said to myself I was just being silly and I closed my eyes. Less than five minutes after closing my eyes, all I remember was my ex-husband saying "It wasn't me" and an almighty bang and sudden halt of the car. A driver on the other side of the road had fallen asleep at the wheel and had hit the car in front of us and it flipped up into the air, landed on our car and when straight off the top of the roof and landed upside down. Miraculously, we were unhurt apart from whiplash. The people in front had cuts from the broken glass and minor injuries. The family of the car that landed on the roof weren't so lucky. The wife had been in the back seat and was thrown from the back window and died instantly and the son had extensive injuries and was in hospital for a number of months afterwards. I remember the horrible eerie silence, there was massive queues of traffic and not a single sound. The fire brigade commented that they were amazed that we were unhurt. We were truly blessed and I knew my father had kept us safe and protected. Especially as a few weeks later I discovered I was pregnant with my second son.

What's death got to do with love I hear your brain churn? I felt it was important to share, my father's passing. This was where I lost my trust and lost my flow in life and the love of me as I know part of me died with him.

When we understand death we can understand that it is just the end of a chapter, when we love someone so much on the physical plane your love is transported to the spiritual plane too love has no boundaries, love never dies.

Understanding that love exists all the time with no boundaries allows us to tap in to the love vibration and that we are always connected to our loved ones and diminishes the pain of them not physically being around. We can keep that love with us and not let the death define us.

Death isn't as final as we think, often it's a new beginning and that is trust!

Our loved ones are as much as a breath away, when we allow ourselves to connect back to our physical body and be in our body we can hear, sense and feel.

Death is only one way in which we come out of the flow of love.   Trauma, loss of trust between friends or lovers are some of the other ways in which our disconnection happens.

My divorce felt like a death, as the person who I had loved was wrenched away and the deception of a friend was a real blow!   But the real blessing was finding me and realising my love for me was still there and I worked on strengthening that.   I had trust and faith in myself.

Trust

We all know what trust is.   We know that it's a faith we put in people that they wouldn't do anything to hurt or harm us. Trust is very fragile and can be easily broken. It can take a long time to regain trust in a person again, for some, it may never be regained.

You can trust people and not have an emotional love for them and equally love someone emotionally and have no trust. Trust is showing a vulnerable side of yourself and believing that the person will be respectful to your vulnerability, have your best interests at heart and honour the sacredness of you.

When you trust in the divine, you put your faith in the angels, universe or god that you will be heard and your answers and fears are heard and guidance provided for your highest good.

My trust grows every day, through small things to big things. One of my biggest trusts that I had was when I opened up my Complementary Healthcare Practice. I trusted the angels to help attract clients to me and for my clinic to grow. I opened up my clinic with very little money, I was a single parent and relied on myself to provide for my family. My fears were alleviated and right from day one, my clinic grew and grew and still grows. What still amazes me to this day, is how people stumble upon my clinic and when they come for treatment, they always end up answering other questions they have about their life. My services appear at the right time, my treatments become blended with others and spiritual insights thrown in for good measure too! Now that's trust!! I am truly blessed to have a job that I love.

Spiritually, it makes me grow and develop on a daily basis and that I can share and help others to grow too.

Take a few moments and ask yourself these questions

- Who do you trust?
- Do you trust yourself?
- Can you trust in the divine?
- If someone breaks your trust, can you forgive and trust again?

Fear

We mentioned earlier that our bodies only know love and fear. Love is a high vibrational energy that radiates out and attracts love and loving situations positivity and the good to us. So what then is fear? Fear in the negative aspect which stops the love from flowing, human nature and conditioning allows for fears to develop. We have all commented on how kids are fearless they have no inhibitions, they just accept what is, they do not judge.

Fear teaches us to move into love if we chose to do so. Fear can be the catalyst to move us from our comfort zone. So yes, fear is the negative side, however we need it to propel us forward in our life or we become stuck!

Some people live there life consumed in fear, the fear is always in the future it has never happened nor likely to because they fear it, it's an illusion. It's the part of the ego of the mind creating an images of what may or may not happen often there is no foundation to base the fear on. It is as if the mind is playing tricks, which to a certain extent it is, the ego the mind the logical part has kicked in and over ruled the heart, when in actual fact the heart is really smart and knows more. It connects to our higher self and knows what is best for us it's our choice as to whether we follow our heart or our mind!

Opening up spiritually allows for you to switch from working and living life through the logic of the mind to work from the heart, to listen to our heart and act from the heart. As we begin to open our heart to love, joy and increase our trust, miracles do begin to happen.

You hear of miracle stories of how cancer patients make miraculous recoveries! How does that happen, simple they let go of fear? They accept their fate and decide to live positively and the fear goes as the inevitable stares them in the face in most cases that is there worst fear, death, and nothing is worse than that. As the flow of love begins to return, as can life back in to the body. Not everyone chooses to let go of fear and that's ok too as that is what they have chosen. The book *Dying to be Me* by Anita Moorjani explains just that. This woman describes how she had to physically, mentally and emotionally died inside and had a near death experience to realise she had a second chance at life and this time, to live it the way that SHE really wanted to and let go of her fears.

The meditation below works best if someone reads it to

you or you record it and play it back. Take your time don't rush enjoy the loving vibration of the meditation. Enjoy!

Love Meditation

If you can place rose quartz crystals beside you or around you during this meditation to help amplify the love vibration.

When you are ready, close your eyes. Take a deep breath, filling all of your lungs and your stomach, hold for a few seconds............ and breathe out through your mouth.

Letting go of all the cares, worries and stresses of the day and of the week.

Take another deep breath in filling your lungs, feel your chest expand as you breathe in the love, breathe out through your mouth.

Feel all the muscles of your body relaxing, down your arms and fingers....... down your legs and your toes.

Now as you relax deeper, focus your attention on your heart and heart chakra, feeling the energy around this area.

Bathe the heart chakra in a green and a pink colour of light, feel the energy of these colours as it opens up your heart gently.

Feel the heart chakra open up like a lotus flower.

Feel the loving energy as it opens, feel this love surround and nurture your body, feel how this love makes your whole body, allow your body to blend with the love vibration, enjoy!

Now expand this love out into the room, feel it vibrate with the energy and love vibration of the rose quartz, feel the connection between you and the crystal.

This feeling of connection and joy and peace is how love should feel. You now have the ability to link into this feeling at any time, where there are no cares no worries no judgement just a heavenly feeling,

 You are enjoying the moment, the moment that is you.

You hear the mantra "I love myself", "I love myself" playing over and over as you tune in it becomes louder and more powerful "I love myself".

Feel the words wash over you and cleanse your whole being. The words resonate on a deep subconscious level. Feel the love of yourself as it cleanses your cells of your body.

Love now has a new meaning of unconditional love, for yourself and others. Love is love of yourself not found in others or material possessions.

I will leave you for a few moments as you enjoy the peace and serenity of this time.

(Long pause)

It is now time to journey back, you bring this loving feeling back with you.

Feel your energy draw in from the room, back into your body keeping the loving vibration with you.

As you begin to return, feel the flow of energy back into your body, wiggle your fingers and toes and when you are ready open your eyes.

How did that make you feel? Warm and fuzzy? Good! Remember to go back to this meditation at any time you feel as though you have lost the vibration or flow.

I love myself, truly, madly, deeply do, I do!

How often do you wake up in the morning and tell yourself I love you?

Not very often, but why should we not. If we can't love ourselves unconditionally how can we expect others to do the same! We simply can't.

I mentioned earlier how we need to love ourselves, but how do we do that?

One way is to let go of judgement. Easy? WRONG!

Society sparks off judgement, judgement of situations to let us assess if it's safe or not is required to a degree, but the real judgement is the one that we have to judge others before we know them. How often have you judged someone then felt bad because you got them completely wrong? Because your perceptions and your judgements stopped you from seeing clearly.

Love is not just an emotion, it's a way of life, a vibration an energy and understanding and knowing.

Our bodies only know two vibrations: love and fear, positive and negative.

Love and positivity keeps us flowing and keeps the vibration high and attracts more of the same to us.

When fear and negativity comes in, it places blocks in our path and stops the flow and then before we know it, we are attracting more negativity and it blocks us and a vicious cycle begins, until we can allow the positivity back in.

We live in a society where love is given but only with conditions. "I will love you if you promise to ONLY love me!!" Where in fact people's perception of love needs to change. We are capable of loving everybody and everything unconditionally, no conditions attached. Conditions show fear is there.

When you shift your perception you see the world in a much different way, you realise that the actions of another is normally not always but largely down to a lack of love and they don't know how to love or what it feels like to be loved. When you recognise this, it changes the energy and the "judgement" that's been created.

Can you imagine what it must feel like to not know love and what it feels like?

Take for example the wee boy in the playground that is classed as a bully, so he can get some attention, but when you look into the bigger picture, you discover they have a mother that lacks interest in the child and lies in bed all day leaving the kid to see to themselves and the father...well, they are nowhere to be seen! Do you not think the child would respond differently in life, if they had parents or parent that showed them love, hugged them, engaged in conversation with them, played games with them or simply told them they loved them!

We often tend to jump and label people without looking at the reasons why they might be behaving in certain ways.

Often the love has gone or was never there to start with and fear is the only thing they know. That must be a really scary, maybe the parent is scared to and doesn't know how to love or scared they let themselves love the child too much and are then rejected, fear has taken hold. As the saying goes "It is better to have loved and lost, than to never have loved at all".

When we love and are in the flow of love, the vibration

radiates out, touching others that in turn can change their vibration, then the love has a knock on effect. Likewise negativity can pull your vibration down.

There will always be negative people around and its realising you can't change them - they have to want to do that - but you can send loving thoughts and energy to them. Then it's up to them if they wish to make the required changes to be more positive. Remember though, if you are in the unfortunate position to be surrounded by negative people protect yourself in your bubble of white light.

Negativity is quite easy to detect when you begin to understand energy. Negative people or situations have a heavy black feeling and often make you feel uncomfortable especially if you are more positive person.

When we work on ourselves and love and trust our self, we can change the situations round about us. As we open up and connect with our self, it touches those around us. Imagine how life in our world would be if we could all love our self. We seem to think it's wrong to love our self or egotistic, it doesn't need to be like that. Love comes from within then we can attract the right people into our life, the right situations, the desires of life are magnetically drawn towards us.

Gratitude and Love

Gratitude is attitude as the saying goes and it's a good one to follow and practice at the end of the day to express gratitude to all things in your life.

Family, possessions, jobs, lessons learned, friends, without all of these they would not have moulded you into the person you are today, providing the experiences, or the value of your life that you currently have. By expressing gratitude you are acknowledging progress and not just taking things for granted.

Gratuity vibrates high and resonates well with the flow of love.

It bodes well to appreciate all that we have, there is no written law that says all is given! If that was the case, we would all be the same and where would the fun in that be.

So tonight, put time aside for all that you are grateful for in your life.

My gratitude letter to date would be:

"Thank you angels and the universe for all that you have given me in my life to date. My beautiful children that are my world, my mother for her help support and friendship. For all my dear friends that are unique in their own special way and the bonds that we have with each other. Thank you for the opportunities created to help me grow as an individual. Thank you for the experiences I've had, although some may not have been pleasant, they have taught me lessons. Above all, I am grateful for you

showing and guiding me and allowing me to be myself and all that I can be."

It's a really lovely exercise to do and allows you to fully appreciate all the good that's in your life and all that you have achieved.

At the end of each day, take a few moments to be grateful for all that the day has provided, for the smile the woman on the street gave you, for the angels helping you with the parking space you requested, to share in the joy of another's happiness.

Words have power and can pack a mean punch if you say things maybe you didn't truly mean. Be careful what you say to others and as your Granny used to say, be careful what you wish for!

Gratitude really does help us keep in the flow of the universe. It opens up to attract the right vibrations to us.

An exercise that you can do daily is to write down five things you are grateful or thankful for. The more gratuity that's shown in your daily life, the more it pulls towards you. Even in the hardest of times there is always something to be grateful for, which when we are caught up in the middle of the hardest of times, we forget, as we focus on the negative aspect of the situation.

Life passes us by day after day. How often do we stop and notice the small things in OUR lives. Do you notice the newly sprung shoots of the daffodils or the sprinkle of snow on the hills in the distance? Do you hear he sparrows that come regularly around you? It is the smallest of things in life that give us the greatest of pleasures just like kids with cardboard boxes. As your heart chakra opens and begins to see the vastness that awaits you, your perception opens and blossoms and you see visually from the heart so much more.

Song of the Heart

As the heart opens up like a lotus flower and the flow of love runs throughout our lives, our synchronicities of nature connects us to the earth and we feel a real connection with all things. Being in the moment is effortless and allows our bodies and our minds to be free. In these moments our connection to spirit, higher consciousness and the angels are at its greatest. We listen with ease and grace at the guidance we are given to make our daily lives simple and free flowing. We let go of the difficulties we let go of the past that embroils us and realise that the past is where it is and where it remains. The pleasure of the present moment is far greater and we see the beauty in everything we touch and see, as often we miss this when we were caught up in the past or too focused on the future.

As our heart opens and unfolds, we connect with the

space around us that we are now in touch with and we can now join in and dance with the angels and communicate with them on a daily basis. We can join in and sing with the angels on their rays of light. This isn't just our heart that we have opened up and connect to, it's the heart of the universe.

Our journey through the chakras is leading us to the higher consciousness moving from the physical realities of life to the lighter spirit and psychic connection of our mind. It's from our heart that we can connect and we can see our own past lives and future life's also, if we chose to tap into this part of us. Our minds really do have that innate ability to allow us to do this. When we have an understanding of lifetimes gone by it allows us to understand the present and provide us with answers for the present.

We are now at the part in our journey where we understand life is so much more and so much greater than we first thought. Life we now see through completely different eyes. We see and understand anger, hurt, sadness and illness differently. We can look beyond the logical way of thinking and see the spiritual side and lack of spiritual connection in some and see how they are struggling. We have a greater empathy now. Negativity and negative people distance themselves from us and we begin to lack tolerance of negative behaviour.

We can see the heart is much more than an organ for keeping us alive on the physical side of life. It's our doorway to the spiritual realms this is where our sixth sense operates from. Our sixth sense allows for us to connect and feel energy. As we develop that and work with it, we can learn to read situations, feel presences such as spirit and angels we trust the information we get and not dismiss it as if our minds are playing tricks. As I mentioned in the root chakra about angels being around and their signs they give, they will begin to intensify.

As I got into writing this book I became stuck, and I read Sonia Choquette's book *Ask your Guides*. I had this book on my shelf for a number of years, then as I read it there was a part she had written about a student she had named Heather, my ears pricked up more intensely now and she spoke of how Heather had always said she was going to write a book someday but had got stuck and didn't know what to do! I really was flabbergasted at what I was reading. What a coincidence, just as I was feeling stuck! I took her advice and asked Archangel Raphael for help, as you have gathered I became unstuck, what a divine inspired message I received. I just goes to show you when your heart is open and you trust and believe the answers will be given.

As I journeyed to here, I found my heart and my head clearer, I no longer had the chatter in my head my instincts and my intuitive side developed quickly. It wasn't easy clearing the heart to open up especially when I had experienced so much heartache. It would have been easier to keep my guard up and give up, I hate to think what state I would be in If I had went down that road.

Another sign that I was on the right path!

My spirit is soaring high, I have peace, love and joy in my heart, I feel I am at home now and I feel content with all that I have and all that I am.

As your heart opens up a like a lotus flower opening up to the sun, your heart does the same, it's the door way to the spiritual and angelic realms, it is at our heart the angels greet us and welcome us to connect with the universe.

Heart Centre

So how do we get into our heart centre? This is so simple to do, it's as simple as breathing! Three deep breaths that you can hear will bring you to your heart centre, back into your body. When you have done that, focus on love and it radiate out. The heart gives off a magnetic field and it's this field that touches others that come into your energy. The love vibrational energy is high and lower vibrations can on come up and match that vibration, so really your heart can have a pull on someone!

The energy that is love, has the power to make miracles happen. Love really can heal the world if we put our mind to it. When we think about the tragedy of Princess Diana, dying we are all tinged with sadness and this mass consciousness could be felt. Her memorial site is such a sad place to be and this can be felt and even invoke tears to those that visit, due to the mass consciousness of grief that was directed to that site. If a tragedy can cause such sadness to be felt by others, then love spread by a mass consciousness of people can make significant changes to our world that we live in.

Gregg Braden has done significant work in spreading the scientific work of the energy of the heart and working with the Institute of HeartMath should you want to read more on this type of work. Two of the wow pieces that I recall, was how the global satellites' that measure the magnetic pull of the earth. During the time of the attack of the twin towers in 2001, there was a significant increase in the magnetic pull, 15 minutes after the first tower was hit. This was due to the enormity of what had just been witnessed round the world and the mass love that pour from the vast majority of humans at the one time.

The other wow piece was when he was talking about three doctors from a hospital in Beijing, where rather than using the conventional western approach to health, what they used was the power of the heart. The video showed a woman who had terminal cancer of the bladder and how the three doctors by opening up their hearts removed the cancerous tumour in 2 minutes 40 seconds (all captured in real time), the doctors trained how to open their hearts and reach a reasonable magnetic field out-put. It's amazing what can be done, just through love.

When we are in our heart centre we allow ourselves to be in the now and in the present moment. It's easier to let go of the past and not worry about the future. It allows us to be filled with joy. When we are in the flow of love from our heart centre, our life is rich and abundant in every way. Life as we know it takes on a whole new concept and we allow ourselves to see the bigger picture of all that is.

When we are connect through our heart, we feel back to our roots and do what's naturally instinctive to us: we know where we truly belong.

The energy of love allows us to be ourselves to be independent and dependant on ourselves our connection to others is pure connection no ulterior motive. Our love of our self, nurtures and protects us and creates bonds with others that are unique, as the love of each other supports and grows into something new propelling each other on their spiritual journeys though this life time.

Bringing ourselves back to this point keeps us in the present moment in the here and now. It keeps our awareness of many aspects to the present moment. It allows our mind to become still. It's in this stillness that we connect with our heart building the bridge between our heart and our head. When we can be in this stillness we can really hear what our heart tells us and from this point we can find out true souls purpose and what direction in life we need to take. When we learn to trust this information that comes from deep within, then life begins to flow as it should. We are less resistant to what life throws at us. Even in the hard times when we breathe we can see why the lesson has come up and what we need to learn from.

It's only recently that the connection to the heart and its importance had come to light. The science is now backing up how powerful an organ our hearts are. It's not just for pumping blood round out body it gives of an electromagnetic field that is palpable by others and can be felt millions of miles away, when we connect in with another loved one. This reinforces the fact that we are indeed all connected to the same source.

Can you imagine or even comprehend how different our entire world would be if we all connected back into the source of love? If every single one of us took three breaths and came back into the present moment. If we all breathed from our heart and followed out heart!

The material items people think they need would be no more. We would find the happiness that we are searching for. Imagine finding that it already existed inside of you! It's there, we just need to access it and know how to, which I have explained and how simple it can be. Can it really be that simple? Yes!

Connections

Connections come from the heart. When we are in the flow of love we feel connections greatly, especially when they are coherent and match, like when we meet a new mate or life partner.

But there is one connection that is so great that cannot be

broken and it is that of a mother and child. The bonds and connection between mothers are children are so incredible.

I know myself being a parent I often pick up and actually feel what's going on with my sons. Mothers and children are telepathic between each other. This is not a myth and there are many evidence based readings to support this.

When you have that unconditional bond with your child, your heart is open and intuition speaks volumes. I recently experienced this with my eldest son. I felt anxious and agitated and I didn't know why! I was on a course at the time and he had text me to tell me he was changing his mind about an important life decision, however the text and the tone of the text didn't sit well with me. There was a tension that evening and when we chatted about his decision and I was straight with him, I told him what I thought were his concerns and reasons for changing his mind. He looked at me in surprise and said I was right that was exactly how he felt (don't know who got more of the surprise). I was tapping into emotions and feelings he didn't know I knew about in him.

Anyway, the next morning I text him put my feelings out there and thoughts and told him to think carefully before he made a final decision. The text came back and I could feel the anger and the battle that he was having in his mind and he was going to change his direction. As much as he knew it wasn't right and not true to him. Later that day, I was being worked on at the course I was on and I felt a change and a peace inside me, a contentment which I couldn't explain. I checked my phone and he had text to say he had changed his mind again and was going to follow the path that he chosen originally. It as in that moment that I realised just how connected that we were.

So mothers if you are experiencing emotions that you don't quite understand or fit with you, check in with your children. You're tapping into them and their thoughts and maybe, the right word or phrase and offering will be in the right moment.

There is a wonderful video trending on social media just now where the kids are blindfolded and have to find their mother. How they do it is amazingly heart-warming to see. They sense through energy and recognition of their mother's energy, every child finds there mother first time.

As we bring the heart chakra to a close, its worth discussing here about empaths. What's an empath? An empath is someone who feels emotions deeply. They often are able to feel other people's pain when they are within their energy fields. Empaths are highly sensitive and tap into their intuition. This happens when the heart chakra is open, they feel through the heart and often the sacral chakra.

I was into my 30's before a truly understood and realised I was an empath. I could feel other people's emotions and however I didn't know that not everyone felt that! I thought it was normal. I was able to sense how people were feeling and where their aches and pains were without being told. This became more apparent when I done my reiki courses. So much so now I don't like crowds I don't like going to the supermarket at times when its busy I prefer to go when it's quiet. Watching things on the TV and I can feel the pain or the emotions. I don't watch the news very often as it portrays negative stories.

Crystals to use for the Heart Chakra

- Rose Quartz

- Quartz clear

- Emerald

- Jade

- Labradorite

- Moonstone

- Peridot

- Pink tourmaline

Essential oils to balance the Heart Chakra

- Bergamot
- Jasmine
- Lemon
- Rose
- Neroli
- Sandalwood

Message from the Angels

To give love is great, to receive love back is greater it amplifies the energy of love and connects to the heavens above.

Love is a continuum that exists between all worlds past, present and future. When we give love to the universe we receive love back, enhancing our vibration, allowing life to be shown to us in new ways, increasing our awareness perception and intuition. We all possess these abilities it's now so time to use them. It forces us all to be united in love. War teaches us that humanity reaches out and that love, compassion and empathy exist between us all every race, every religion. There is no distinction we are all one.

Love, Energy, creation = New beginnings

When we go inside our hearts and expand into the depths of the unknown, the greater wisdom and knowledge is learned. *We have so much inside us already, we just need to tap into it and use it more. Guidance is there if you choose to follow your TRUE heart. When we go against the grain the restrictions and negativity creep in taking you off course. Sometimes this is necessary to learn, sometimes its pure procrastination. Get into the flow of love, stay positive and focused, keep in the joy and happiness will always be.*

Throat Chakra

The throat chakra not surprisingly is found at the throat area on the neck. The colour associated with this chakra is blue. This chakra connects to the communication part of us. Not solely speaking but in every way we communicate through speech, written word, energy and with spirit the angels and our higher self.

The chakra governs the throat, thyroid, ears and lungs and interestingly in particular the thyroid that the chakra governs is shaped like a butterfly! Why is this interesting, well the butterfly symbolises transformation. The throat chakra is where the transformation takes place as it allows us to communicate freely to create change but more importantly allows us to be honest with ourselves.

Communication is a massive part of our life and is happening continually through how we speak to each other and how we feel and sense. Our bodies are amazing multifunctional vehicles that we have chosen to experience.

Through reiki, my experience of this chakra is that the energy is generally low. We as humans are not the best at communicating and expressing our feelings. I personally had issues with my throat chakra, particularly when I was younger and I didn't express myself, I was always quiet and introvert and constantly had tonsillitis up until my twenties when I stood my ground more and stepped into being me.

The tonsillitis recurred again some years later towards the end of my marriage, when I was experiencing differences in the energies between us and noticing things were different in the way he was towards me. Until I vocalised my thoughts, I never had it again. Some years later it reoccurred when I was in a situation at work where things were uncomfortable and I was being taken advantage of for my kindness however my advantage at that point was that I recognised that this was down to me not communicating and verbalising my emotions. I was stuffing them down and inevitably, I suffered for it.

That for me was a real lesson on the importance of expressing your feelings and not bottling them up. This is where I learned to begin speak my truth!

The throat chakra contains a lot of energy and is often the last one that becomes balanced and when we worked from the heart and followed our guidance the sheer roar from inside us enough to propel us forward in life.

Truth

What is it that we mean when we say truth?

Your truth is different from my truth so who is right? The answer is both are right. We all have different understandings and perceptions making truths different but what really matters is that we are true to *ourselves* that's the key. When we can't be true to our self, the truth we live is in a life of lies. If we can't be true to ourselves, how can anyone else be true to us? You become unhappy, as you do things to suit others which only leads to disappointment and a feeling of disconnection.

Truth is another word for opinions, we all have them doesn't make anyone's opinion any less valid than the next.

Truth is hard because we try to fit into other people's definition of truth and it doesn't work and we tie ourselves up in knots trying to please others. We don't speak up and say what we really think or feel - we try to second guess and say what we think others want to hear. Sound familiar? Well make today be the day that you step out and change that. Be YOU! If someone asks you something and you're not happy then say no, no need to apologise or explain yourself as you are being honest and true to your needs and it will feel good. When we streamline our life and do what we want, life becomes full of opportunities that previously would have been missed and your being shines as life is now creating in the way you want it to.

Truth becomes tricky as it's one of these situations that everybody is right and everyone's opinion has come from a different perspective. What you really need to do is to understand the intent that is behind the truth. Often we take things at face value and it's not until we delve deeper, that we get more of an understanding of things and why they have come to that conclusion of the truth. Often people have the right intent and say the right thing but unfortunately don't follow through. This is when people try to people please and lose their identity.

I had a young girl come to my clinic as her mum was at her wits ends with her behaviour. She was sitting up late at night not wanting the television turned off and acting up, not doing as she was told (yes normal kids' stuff I hear you cry) but when we did some reiki, things came to the surface as I tapped into her energy, I sensed she was open to spirit! When I put my hands on her head at the beginning of the session, there was an army of people standing with her - it's was incredible...no wonder she was playing up! The poor soul was seeing spirit and was lost and scared as she didn't understand it. After her initial session things calmed down as I had advised her and her mum to do the protection technique to help protect her and asked her to ask the spirits not to bother her at night time. The following week her mum had noticed a massive change in her and she was no longer trying to fit in. She was comfortable enough to be able to talk about what was happening and didn't feel so "abnormal" as she realised there are others that has special gifts like hers. Her decision now was to either work with or understand the spirit world or whether to close it off completely.

Although the following weeks were up and down as revelations about her guardian angel came to light that over whelmed her, she rebelled as she didn't know if this was the path she wanted to take at this time. She now had to decide to continue on this path or close it off for the time being.

She stepped into her truth and wasn't trying to comply to be someone that she wasn't. Her behaviour was a direct result of her feeling isolated and unable to speak her truth and allow herself to go more with the flow and let go of the need to control.

Communication

Being the throat chakra communication is very important. Communication is vital in our life so we can express ourselves and get ourselves out of danger but have we ever thought, how do we actually communicate?

- We can be verbal and use our voice

- We can write and express our self

- We can use energy!

Use energy, she must be off her head! How do you communicate with energy? We have all used and experienced body language...right? How often are the words that are said, backed up more by the body language? We have all experienced saying one thing and meaning another and picked up on it.

The energy vibration behind things we saying actual is picked up and sensed by us more than what we actually say.

When you add feeling into things it intensifies its meaning and power.

Like I mentioned before, when you look in the mirror and tell yourself you love yourself do you say it in a way that it is really chirpy, positive and happy or monotone, humdrum and depressing?

Which are you most likely to respond too? Well your body responds the same.

The butterfly is a magnificent creature. It teaches us how to transform from one thing to the next and that change is beautiful and brings us back to our feelings. It creates new feelings, new energies and new experiences but how we perceive them is down to us. We can choose to accept love and make the best of the change or we can rebel and feel stuck.

Feelings are important as they transmit a frequency that the universe responds to. This response is the law of attraction. We can all speak positive, but do we mean it? Do we feel the positivity of what we say? No, not always! We spoke earlier about how words have power, what gives them there power, yes you guessed... how we feel!

So let's look more at the Law of Attraction as mentioned in the solar plexus. When we manifest and ask for that £1 million cheque, do you believe it or do you do what most people do and ask for it and almost instantly say "Oh well, that won't happen soon" or "Like that will ever happen!!" Then you have cancelled your request. How? Because your feelings don't match the vibration of what you have asked for, your internal GPS gets the request lost in transmission.

If you put your order in of receiving a £1 million cheque and actually believed that it was now on its way to you and you visualise your bank balance statement displaying £1,000,000, your feelings are different and you know you are worthy of that money. You know how you will spend the money as you visualise the dream car, dream house and accessories or your dream holiday and you can actually feel and see yourself with these items, you pull it closer towards you into your energy.

An example for me was when I wanted to move and expand my business. I knew I wanted something bigger with less noise but I knew I wanted to stay on the same street, the clinic was already on.

The process of this happening began by being at my friend's parents' house for a birthday party and there I met her dad's friend and other family members.

The following week I decided to go across the road and look at a property that I knew had been empty, but I knew it was also quite big, bigger than I anticipated, but I thought hey! No harm in looking.

Yes the initial unit I had went to look at was too big, but low and behold there was a unit next door, which I never knew about and I was surprised it was empty. From the outside, it looked perfect. I was unsure of how many rooms there were or how big they were so I decided to call the number. The landlord confirmed there were three rooms which I thought and would be perfect, so I arranged to meet him an hour later.

The landlord arrived and I couldn't believe it! It was my friend's dad's friend who I had met the week before, which at the time, I had no idea was a landlord!!!

I came in the rooms were perfect size, excellent light still on the same street, but gave me more quietness. There on the mat at the door was two white feathers, just to confirm it was ok.

The move went ahead and I came to another sticking point. I was already tied into a lease in the current shop!

However, I knew the new place was for me. I kept my focus and vision and I could see me in the new place and it came to the weekend I was moving out and I still hadn't found anyone to fill the current tenancy of the old shop, but I kept going nothing was holding me back.

Then the day I was opening the new shop, someone came to view the old shop and loved it and signed the new tenancy and again for them there was a single white feather in the hallway, which wasn't there before. How divinely guided and blessed I felt and a further confirmation all was as it should be.

My point! I manifested my shop. I put out the requirements and the universe guided me to it, I felt, I believed, I trusted and I was guided.

We create what we think. Its having our words and feelings matching that attracts them to our reality. I believed I already had it I envisioned myself already there.

When you understand and realise this process, you can change your life. You are more conscious about the words that you chose, positivity attracts, having said that in some situations where you are in a negative state or place in your life, knowing that you can change it allows you to dream the positive outcome allowing change to happen, the polarity of each draws you to a balance in your life. Just as you can't experience light without dark or day without night. Without each other you can't experience the one without the other.

So if we want to communicate with spirit, angels or our higher self, we have to be positive and give out the right message. We have to be clear in our intent of what we want to communicate. We are in control of spirit communication and if at any time we feel uncomfortable we can ask for spirit to step back.

I've kind of jumped from spirit communication and intuition, this is deliberate as these are things that happen continually without any effort and these are senses we were born with but have lost. This is were being in your heart centre is important as the heart already knows, by bringing ourselves back to the heart centre, we are allowing our heart to remember what it already knows! How cool!! As mentioned before the heart is the centre that connects us spiritually and with reality its where these two worlds meet and connect.

How spirit communicates with us can come in a variety of ways, such as images, sounds, smells, a sense of knowing or a mixture of them all. You will have come across the "clairs" before, meaning clear. Clairvoyance, clairsentience, clairgustance, clairaudience, clairtangency (psychometry) and channelling or trance.

There is no right or wrong way to get information, it's

whatever is your strongest sense. Some get a mixture of them all.

Communication with spirit often feels different to your intuition! Spirit communication is dropped into you mind like an email using which ever sense. There's no question of doubt - you say what you get, how could you know what someone's granny was called or looked like, let alone what her last words to you were? I had an opportunity to attend a trance and physical mediumship course. The first part was doing a trance meditation, allowing you to go deeper and letting go, until your consciousness is pushed aside and your body is used as a vessel for spirit to communicate through you. I remember once I had reached that point I felt my body was if it were massive ten times the size, I felt a rush of anxiety and my heart racing and I started to speak! I can't remember what it was that I said as they weren't my words but they seemed to have an impact. Later we were in a cabinet were you sit in darkness with a very dim light on you. I was sitting there I was aware of what others were saying as I went into the trance state and hear people gasping and saying "Oh my goodness", apparently a lot of faces flashed in front of mine. One woman recognised them as members of her family, finally the face that settled over mine was her mother. The words I relayed to her were the last words her mother spoke to her before she passed away! I had never met this woman before. She was so grateful. I was in a state of exhilaration and shock at what had just happened. Not bad for my first trance experience.

Intuition is a feeling. It can ripple through your body and you often get a knowing that something feels right or wrong as you grow spiritually you learn to trust this feeling and it stops you from taking wee detours in life. Although there will be times you don't listen and go against the grain and that's ok to as sometimes you have to make the mistake to learn from. Life is a big learning curve, we choose to make it easy or hard for ourselves.

With this meditation, don't rush it. Take your time and really feel the energy working and clearing. This is your communication chakra allow it to release and let go.

Throat chakra Meditation

Play some soothing music in the background.

Close your eyes take a nice long deep breath in, really fill your lungs and abdomen and then let it all go....

Take another deep breath in and feel your body relax, feel all the muscles relaxing and letting go.

Feel all the areas of stress and tension releasing, feel your body just melt away into your chair.

Imagine your body being filled with light, lightening all the dark areas in your body, feel your energy becoming lighter, fading away all the cares, worries and stress allowing your body to just simply be.

(Pause)

Now take your attention to your throat chakra feel the intensity of the colour blue, notice what shade of blue, does the energy feel open, light and free flowing or heavy and constricted.

Stay here for a while and focus on the chakra and the energy there until it feels free and light. Don't worry if you cough or feel your throat irritated - this is ok it's the energy moving and clearing.

(Long pause...........)

Knowing now that the energy at the throat chakra is clear and open, you can step forth and speak your truth being open and honest with yourself. You express yourself freely in the knowledge that you are clear. You are aware of the shift that has happened here you feel the energy vibrating and radiating through you as you speak true of yourself of your body and mind, give thanks.

When you feel ready, begin to bring your awareness back into the room and where you are sitting.

Note down your feelings visions and thoughts in your journal.

Letting Go

Letting go isn't always easy. It affects the throat chakra

the most as this is the channel for communication and voicing ourselves even if it's for nobody else to hear just letting the words and feelings to come up can create such a sense of achievement and clear the internal pathways inside allowing energy to flow more easily.

The concept that our feelings and emotions create illness and disease is a lot for our mind to comprehend, but when you begin to understand how emotions affects us, you can see the impact in our health.

With colonic hydrotherapy being one of the treatments that I do, I see a number of clients that suffer from constipation and they are at their wits end, as they have tried everything but the constipation begins to rule their life. After I have went through the basics like diet and water consumption and other things, I ask how their mind feels. Does it feel congested? I often get funny looks and when they think about it then issues of resentment or grief tend to show up.

One client I remember was dismissive of the thought that it was linked to her mind. The treatment was going slow and I asked her a simple question had she been away on holiday? Then the flood gates opened in two ways. She had lost her parents within a short time of each other and was struggling with it emotionally. When she began to talk about it the waste also released and she felt great afterwards. Not only had she got rid of the waste that was inside her, her mind was so much clearer and she realised herself the connection with the mind. Voicing how she was feeling and hearing it aloud help her to have a shift internally.

Don't get me wrong, colonic treatments don't become therapy sessions but sometimes the wee nudge to recognise that the thoughts in your head and your bowel are connected. After all the brain did stem from the bowel! Hence the gut being referred to as the second brain or having that gut feeling.

Letting go seems to be the hardest things to do, it doesn't have to be.

Be consciously aware of what you're holding on to!

Are you ready to let it go? Or another question is, do you want to let it go? What good is it doing you holding on to it?

I had a conversation with a friend recently about letting go and forgiveness. What struck me was the only person now suffering was herself. She was trying to convince herself she had let things go and dealt with the situation and hurt but what was still there, was the anger. In her mind she had dealt with the issue but in reality she had suppressed it. She was horrified at even the thought of forgiveness, she could not see she was now causing her own pain by holding on to it. She had not seen the value of the lesson she had been given, which could result in history repeating itself in time to come.

In her head, she was convinced she had let go as her ego

was letting her think that. The fact that she had to convince herself she had let go was highlighting the need to delve deeper into what was preventing her from letting go and the lessons still had to be learnt.

When you have let go of the situation, person or whatever the issue is it stays at peace. You can talk about it without it causing a reaction or evoking any emotion. However when you have let go truly you will laugh at it and yourself as to why you hung on to it for so long.

Water and Love

Dr Emoto was infamous for the study about positivity and the effects of using water. He used water and rice and many other mediums to test theories out. With the rice, he had three tubs. One was giving loving positive words of encouragement. The second tub was not given any communication. The third tub was given negative words and phrases this was over a thirty day period.

The results concluded that tub one, the positive influence was that the rice was almost still edible after that period of time. The second tub had putrefied in that period without any influence. It essentially had been ignored and rotted and the third tub was two thirds rotten. He demonstrated that even things such as water and rice were influenced by positive words and actions such as love. So if it can make such an impact on water and rice what does the negative chatter in our head actually do to our bodies and the ignorance that we give ourselves and others.

With the water experiment, he froze molecules of water that had been given loving, blessed and gratifying words said and the beauty of the crystals formed were stunning, equally there were water molecules that were given negative and hatred words and the images were ugly and unformed. There are many images on Google to have a look at, it's worth it.

We are made up of water so recall the beauty of the images created by the water molecule and the beauty it creates inside of you. We are all beautiful. We need to believe it and we need to feel it.

So if there is only one thing you take from this book I ask that you speak lovingly to yourself and break the cycle of the harsh judgements we tend to have of ourselves. Words have power, if we can remember that we are half way there.

Speak lovingly to yourself and others, bless the food that you eat as it nourishes you. Again, if we have negative thoughts about what we are eating we are ingesting more negativity. Small changes to the way we think can have a massive impact on ourselves and those around us.

Self-Expression

When we let go and allow ourselves to speak our truth we make a greater connection to the divine. Blocks clear from the throat and allows us to speak freely and listen intently. Our intuition heightens and our trust grows. We have a greater understanding of why things happen, we understand when our negative self-doubt creeps in that it impacts on our life and how we see things, it blurs our judgement.

When we are in balance here our communication with spirit and the Angels grow, we have more freedom of expression. We often can become more aware of the presence around us as the lower chakra energies filter up, our energies meet and we feel elevated. When this chakra is balanced we feel complete. This is normally the last chakra to balance due to the abundance of energy that comes here.

Our bodies

As we move up the chakras and as they become balanced and you become sensitive, you may find that you become more sensitive to food and environmental factors. I remember reading about this and thinking what a lot of tosh! That was until I began working on myself and became aware of how I was beginning to react to certain foods particularly gluten and dairy. I now understand that fruits and vegetables have more energy and are better for my body to cope with and when I eat them my energy is lifted also. Sensitivities are not just connected to your spirituality however when you open your body up to the universe and work with universal energy and light, purposefully you become more aligned with your body and tune in to how it feels you become acutely aware of what's good for you and what's not.

When some of the chakras are out of balance it is beneficial to eat fruit and vegetables that correlate to the colours of the chakras that you are working on. The foods are colourful and normally the benefits of the fruit or vegetables match in with the organs associated to the chakra colour, see even nature helps us out, when we understand the chakras we can see how we can help ourselves with our and mind and through diet.

I have come to listen to my body and what it needs. I am aware of my bodies need for clean eating, in turn this helps raise my energy vibration and allows my senses and intuition to sharpen.

Our intuition is a natural function of our bodies. We are meant to be spiritually aware, psychic and intuitive: it is part of who we are, it's not something unique to certain people but part of our wisdom deep within.

Our consciousness is awakening it's time for us to wake up and take control, let go of the fear let the fun and childlike nature within us surface let our hearts fill with joy and love fill our being with light.

Crystals to help the Throat chakra

- Lapis
- Blue kyanite
- Sodalite
- Turquoise
- Aquamarine

Essential oils for the Throat chakra

- Basil
- Bergamot
- Peppermint
- Cypress
- Chamomile

Message from the Angels

We walk your path of truth close by your side always and forever. Do not carry the burdens of these hurts or life lessons. With the grace of the divine, let them go and free your spirit and your soul. Be ever present in the now release the past and embellish the future. Go forth and speak your divine truth as it is your God given right to do so.

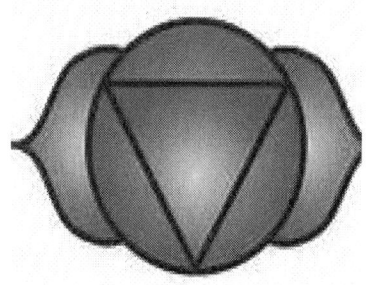

Third eye chakra

The third eye chakra is found in the centre of your forehead in line with your nose. This chakra is linked to vision and your inner visions. This chakra is responsible for what we would call our "sixth sense". It's associated with the colour indigo. It governs more of the intellect, wisdom, insight and knowledge.

As we move up the chakras, greater spiritual insights happen. The third eye allows us to see in the other dimensions.

Have you ever closed your eyes and seen multiple faces or even just one? Often we dismiss them but this is your guide's helpers or spirit communicating with you. As mentioned before, each person has a more dominant sense, for some it's sight/seeing, for others is taste, smells, knowing.

I am more dominant in a knowing and sensing. I am however occasionally seeing. Currently at night when I close my eyes before I drift off I often see wee movie clips, sometimes I am see accidents and how someone has come to pass or I see what lies in the future. Sometimes I know it's concerning me and sometimes I have no idea! This is still in the learning phase for me. I am fortunate to have many wonderful friends that are further developed in their gifts to ask for help.

Monthly at my clinic, I have a psychic surgeon Chris Ratter come and run a healing clinic. I asked him about my strange movie clips. He explained as my light brightens I am drawing spirit closer to me which is allowing spirit to show me things. I am happy at the moment and I'm not frightened by it more intrigued as to what will happen next as life is one big continuing journey for me also.

Meditation is a wonderful way to work with and strengthen the third eye. One experience I had was after a few months meditating and really getting into it I noticed I would get a tight energetic band round my third eye, as if it were expanding. Often I would see an eye opening, which I knew was a vision that the third eye was opening more. The meditations were colourful and vivid as if I was really there.

As I've worked on myself and worked up through my

development through the chakras, my meditations have changed. In the beginning I got lots of colours and symbols, which now I have uncovered the meanings of the symbols with relevance to me. My meditations now give me stillness and peace. If I need an answer, I go within in to the stillness and I'm presented with my answer or solution. The stillness strengthens my light, allows me to be more aligned with my higher self and in tune with my body.

Mediumship

It used to make me always wonder when I went to see a medium or psychic at the conversations they could have and why they would laugh at what they heard or saw. I wished it was me sometimes.

I was doing a mediumship mentoring course and we had to stand as if we were doing platform work. Well! All these images kept filtering into my head and it was like a sketch from Still Game (a Scottish comedy show). I could not work it out so I gave in. I was laughing and put out what I was seeing, Jack and Victor were the comedy names but I was getting the names Paul and Phil and how they were like brothers. It was someone's birthday and the pair of them had a right "banter" between them and were really funny. Turned out there was someone in the group who had a brother Phil who had a friend Paul and were indeed just like these characters that were on TV. They had just been speaking to them earlier that morning as it was the brother's birthday! Everyone was laughing at the humour that spirit was bringing across. This sound and energy vibration strengthens the link with spirit.

The difficulty with mediumship is that when you get images you have to interpret what you're getting. That's why practice is important to really understand how your communicators who work with you.

Once doing reiki, I saw Annie from the musical! Annie was my favourite movie when I was younger much to my sister's annoyance as it was on constant repeat! Anyway I couldn't work it out again, so I stopped analysing and just asked the client if the name Annie meant anything to them, and it did. It was a grandparent…brilliant but then the image was getting stronger, so what they were telling me was that she was a character just like Annie from the movie and had red hair and liked to singing. So, you see spirit was giving me images that I could identify with to get over the information that was needed. This started happening more and more. I often get meaningful songs too, which can have their own message to the recipient.

We are all born with this unique gift but we lose it throughout the years of society influencing right and wrong. But really who is right and who is wrong?

Learning to trust yourself as we have been learning through the chakras as it opens you up to a whole new world, or universe rather.

Spirituality, healing, mediumship, meditation are all linked together they fit together like a jigsaw. They can't be taught, they have to be learned and everyone's experience is different to the next persons. We can be guided in ways that have helped others and combinations work well for someone else.

I had a friend who was developing as a medium, I was developing spiritually as I was growing from within and learning more about me which opened up my mediumship skills. We would chat and often I would be criticised as I wasn't learning through a church or in a specific way. However the messages I was receiving weren't any less valid that hers. It was sad that she couldn't see that there was more than one way to do something, just like anything in life there is always more than one way to achieve the same goals. One thing with mediumship and messages being given, is always be respectful to the recipient. Messages coming from spirit and angels are always with love and compassion, the energy will be high. If the energy is low it's more likely that your ego has kicked in. In honour of spirit always be honest and true, if you don't get a link that's ok, it's not meant to be, or you're not the right one to give the message required, just don't take it personally. There will be a reason why and it's not up to us to judge it.

I do firmly believe when we work on ourselves we become in tune with our bodies and mind, our intuition heightens. This is regardless of what job you do and want to do, it doesn't have to be mediumship.

I see more people connecting on a soul level. Our souls are becoming awakened, we draw the people we need towards us and life it's self is showing us that we have the power in our own hands. We do indeed have the ability to change the paths ahead of us rather than just mindlessly bumbling along blaming everything else. It takes one change of thought to change your life.

Crystal Cave Meditation

Take three deep breaths….. In and out nice a steady

Feel your body as it begins to relax

Feel you mind begin to still

Imagine in your mind that it's a warm summer's day and in front of you there is a forest with a path winding through.

You begin to walk towards the path and meander on it through to the other side where you come to a clearing.

As you stop and have a look about you see in the distance there is a bridge.

You walk over to the bridge and begin to cross it, half way you stop and look into the still waters.

As you gaze into the water you notice your reflection, you ponder at your gaze for a few moments noticing what's reflecting back, are you happy, sad, disappointed, lonely, contented...do you like what you see?

As the reflection fades you continue over the rest of the bridge.

On the other side a little in front of you there is an entrance to a cave, you walk over and enter the cave.

As you step inside you feel this amazing energy tingle all over your body. The cave is full of crystals you notice the colours you're drawn to you, might even hear the name of the crystal. Stand in this beautiful energy as it heals you, nourishes you and revives you. Feel this energy absorb into you.

Once you feel ready you walk forward in the cave and you see rainbow showers. As you walk through the red, you feel it wash and cleanse you,…… through the orange as it washes and cleanses you, ………through the yellow as it washes and cleanses you………., through the green as it washes and cleanses you ………into the blue as it washes and cleanses you ………. Into the purple as it washes and cleanses you…….. And into the pure brilliant white….

As you step out the rainbow showers, you feel purified as if you've been topped up with love and nothing matters.

You head towards the exit of the cave and as you step out there is a being there to greet you.

They welcome you and ask if you're ready to meet your guides and helpers. You nod and they extend their hand to you and you walk toward the burning open fire. As you sit around the fire, your guides, Angels, helpers, spirit friends or animal totems gather as well. You become acquainted, you recognise the energy and you feel peace.

Sit for the next few moments allow yourself to ask

questions to your guides, helpers all that have come forward.

Ask for their name?

Ask if they have a message for you?

Do they have a gift for you?

As your time comes to an end, thank all that has come forward, thank them for the information, gifts and knowledge. You know that at any time you can return to this special place.

As you get up to leave, the being that greeted you is there. They take you by the hand and lead you to the cave.

Once again you thank the being for taking you to meet your guides.

You step back through the cave, into the rainbow showers through the White the purple the blue and the green the yellow the Orange and the red.

You're back in the crystal room and the abundant energy that's there.

You step out the cave.

Head back towards the bridge. You cross the bridge and again stop halfway, you gaze in the still waters again you see your reflection. This time you notice a change, there's something different about the reflection looking back. There's a twinkle in the eyes, you see your guide's reflection appear in the water, reminding you that they are always near.

The reflections fade.

You know you feel different and that things have changed inside you, you continue across the bridge and into the forest back along the path. At the other side you stand, feeling at peace within.

Take three deep breaths and bring yourself back into the room.

Open your eyes

<3

How do you feel?

That's quite a powerful meditation and good to go back over a few times. It gives you the balance of relaxation and the chance to connect within.

This meditation I often do with my group it's good to go back to. We all love this one as it allows us to access ourselves on a deeper level every time we get something different. It makes us connect to how the outer world sees us rather than how we think the outside world sees us, which can be quite liberating. Connecting with our guides and angels on a more personal and intimate level offering us advice or guidance which is always loving, gives us the jolt on the next step of our journey. It helps our body and mind to be cleared and reset, the worries that seemed huge mountains become small mole hills that we can cope with. Going within allows us to heal physically, spiritually and mentally.

Language of Numbers

I feel deeply connected to numbers and the messages that they bring to me. Just like words, numbers carry a vibration and each number has a unique energy and meaning to them.

It was quite funny when I had thought about writing about numbers and numerology in the book. I had a strange few weeks with numbers talking to me. I get the thought then I need to experience it so I can write about! I surely have been divinely guided in writing.

At one of my groups, I had been talking about 222 and how I had seen the number often recently and how it's commonly interpreted as spirit loved ones being round about, which at that particular time was relevant to me and my circumstances I had going on. Well after group one, of the girls dropped me off and we were chatting and I was pulled to look at the mileage meter and low and behold it had 222 right outside my door! We laughed about it and then ten minutes later, I went into the house and I bought a book on Amazon and checked the bank balance of the account I use for these things. I couldn't believe my eyes the numbers were 111.11. 11 this is an auspicious number and is linked to positivity and guidance by the spirit world and where the physical and spiritual worlds connect and a sign of synchronicity. The fact there were five 1's, there added more kick to it! Fives are about change, wisdom, knowledge and often travel. So after being blown away with that, I was thinking about what had happened. I knew in my head was sure spirit was trying to get my attention, then about another ten minutes later I saw the numbers 555, screaming the changes to me that I had connected into with the 111.11.

There are various ways in which numbers can be analysed. So firstly, I looked at the Doreen Virtue angel number book, always my first go to point and I took on board what was said there, but I knew it still wasn't enough that there was more to it.

There are a few systems to numerology, Pythagoras and Chaldean. Neither is better or worse that the other it's just a matter of preference to which system you use, so I decided to research both systems.

A few days later, I was going from the shop to my home, which is only about ten minutes travel in the car. In that short space of time, I saw 999 222 999 222 999 999 777. Now if that wasn't coincidental what is?! My head was buzzing! My youngest son had a friend in and I took him home and on the short journey there I saw 777 and 777! I knew for definite that there was a deeper message.

Although I have a knowledge of numbers and numerology, I was getting into deeper messages, so I contacted a friend who has more knowledgeable on numbers and was able to decipher my message to me. She worked it out and the message was SIR I.C.U RAJI? This was one of my guides communicating with me through numbers.

For days after, I was seeing sequences of numbers 333 444

444 999 and a lot of it was connecting in with me writing my book as I had slowed down a little on writing it but I was continually being urged to keep going and to get it finished. It was telling me it was so right to be doing it, which was encouraging!

Writing about numbers has also taught me much more about messages and the meaning of numbers. Not just working out life paths, destiny, soul, karmic issues all of which can be worked out using the vibration of numbers created through date of birth and your name.

The numbers in my life show up as 9's and 5's, phone numbers, national insurance numbers, mobile numbers, door numbers, bank account numbers and even insurance numbers. It now makes me chuckle as I often add up numbers and I'm now never surprised that 27/9 is recurrent.

So what numbers show up in your life?

Have you previously been aware of numbers showing up repetitively?

Do you see 11.11 often?

So, how do you notice numbers talking?

As above with the 999, 222 scenario, I saw these on car number plates and my eyes where pulled to them and made me go oh! The 111.11 seemed like it was bold and screamed at me. Sometimes I wake up during the night, look at the clock at strange times, I register the time and it makes me smile. I immediately fall back asleep, I now recognise it as the Angels communicating with me and look the number up in the angel number book in the morning and always always always is relevant to my current thoughts or situation.

When I do oracle card readings that have numbers I often add them together to get a feel for deeper meanings being shown.

Like I mentioned earlier, there are various ways to look at numbers and different systems. I don't want to lead you one way or another however I do hope I have wet your appetite enough to investigate it more to see where numbers occur.

A very general insight in the numbers 1-9 (there will be other interpretations find what fits you)

1   - new beginnings, creation, positivity, will power

2   - relationships, balance, duality, love, harmony, adaptability

3   - past, present, future, creativity, communication, moving forward, manifestation

4   - foundations, security, protection, patience, practicality

5   - change, knowledge, wisdom, instability, travel, life experience

6   - peace, harmony, love, healing, protection, seeing

7 - spirituality, soul searching, wisdom, silence, trust

8 - success, flow of life, power, self-reliance

9 - end of a cycle or chapter, tying up loose ends, universal love, compassion, magnetism, strengthening, humanitarian

Have fun exploring numbers and what deeper meanings they bring to your life. One book that might be of interest is Hilary H Carter *11.11: The Story of the Convent*. This is a fascinating book as to how numbers lead this woman on a journey to buy a convent in Spain and all the synchronicity that happened along the way and other hidden meanings using numbers in history.

Psychic Awareness

What is psychic awareness? Well, as we have worked through the chakras, psychic awareness is about connecting to ourselves and our intuition and seeing what lies ahead. The clearer we become the more we see and feel, as our 6th sense heightens.

In Greek, the word psychic connects to the psyche of our mind, it connects to natural laws accessing our higher being.

We all have psychic abilities. Some of us try and connect back to our roots doing mediation, grounding exercises or yoga. That's where being connected and aware of us as a being expands our awareness when we can connect with our body it becomes easier to connect with others. This is where our energies blend and communicate and we pick up signals, going back to the sacral chakra. This is also where we connect and link in with a partner as our energies connect first, often this is how we know or feel love at first sight, that is why with sexual relationships they become more intense as the energies blend at a more intimate level and we" feel" the emotions. Our energies go out and feel first and feedback to us, when connected sexually through a partner, you often feel or know when things are wrong. It's your energy feeling for you, so trust what you feel it's never wrong!

Life teaches us so many things. We are guided along the way. We choose the life we lead, I hope so far this book has allowed you to see the benefits of choosing positivity in guiding you forward. We can avoid much of the negative aspects if we seek the positivity, the kindness and gratitude our life can bring. In the darkest of time we are offered the smallest chink of light. We can either choose to follow the light or not.

I want you to be able to realise you are the master of your own ship and you can make the changes to turn your life around, I did and so have many others and so can you. Believe in yourself, believe in the magic that's inside you.

Life passes us by day after day. How often do we stop and notice the small things in our lives as it's these things that give us the greatest pleasures.

As your third eye opens and you begin to see the vastness that awaits you, your perception opens and blossoms and you see visually and with your mind's eye so much more, beauty and depth.

Crystals for the Third Eye

- Amethyst
- Angelite
- Aquamarine
- Black Obsidian
- Purple Fluorite
- Clear Quartz
- Kyanite

Essential Oils for the Third Eye

- Angelica Root
- Clary Sage
- Frankincense
- Juniper
- Patchouli

- Rosemary
- Sandalwood

Message from the Angels

We communicate to you in many ways, your inner visions are us showing, directing and guiding you forward in all that you do. When you are open you will trust this guidance that we offer to you. Until that point, your ego will interrupt and take you along different paths, some of which you will need to journey on to learn. Feel the peace, feel the love, feel our presence deep within. Be the love <3

Crown Chakra

The crown chakra found at the top of our heads. Connected with the colour white and purity of the divine connections. This is where we truly connect deep within ourselves. All the work of the previous chakras meet here allowing us to feel the 'I am' within us.

We have done so much work to get to here. We have discovered parts of us we didn't know, we have faced fears and found an understanding of who we REALLY are. How privileged it is to have reached this point?

As the chakras balance and you understand yourself more, the deeper inner work is easier to access. There is more of a stillness in our minds and we can really tap into the energy around us. We know how to steer our lives on to a path we desire and use the power of our thoughts and inner dialogue to keep us on the path, we so desire. We realise we really are the navigator to our journey and we can guide our paths and steer clear of the stormy waters.

We now understand life and what it's teaching us. In a bad situations we can see the positive of what we are being taught - maybe not right at the time, but in reflection. Life is so different when we see through the eyes of love and understand the energy of love, how to use it and apply it to our life's.

I AM

I am that, I am. A very powerful statement. I remember hearing it for the first time and not really getting it so to speak. I had read A Course in Miracles and one of the lessons was saying this table does not mean anything, this door does not mean anything, this chair does not mean anything. I duly did the exercise but didn't really connect with the concept.

I had been on a training course and we were shown a video by James Twyman explaining I am that, I am and it hit me in that moment I really understood the power of the short statement. As I breathed into the statement, I felt a rush through me. I could now turn to the chair or table and connect with I am that, not that it didn't mean anything but that it meant more as *I am* that, we are all apart of everything.

Something inside me had changed. I had let go of attachment. Emotions had changed also and at that particular time, I was struggling with life events of my children growing up and evolving. It wasn't a gradual process as I had thought it would be, but more turbulent than I had anticipated and although I am very spiritual and grounded, this really knocked me sideways. I realised that yes I am a mother I nurture and care for my children, however I realised the I AM that *I AM* and that my children are their I AM, they are individuals in their own right. We as parents are just for guidance and protection and they are on their journeys in life and have to learn their lessons. The I AM that I now understood so profoundly changed all that, I was in the right place at the right time connecting with information I already had knowledge of, but now understood in a new revolutionary way and that was a true blessing.

Dr Wayne Dyer writes in many of his books that I AM is the only constant in our lives. Our bodies change from babies, toddlers, teenagers, adults, seniors but the only constant is the I AM. Have a think about that. He explained then, that our bodies are then only an illusion, which was a game changer for me! We really are spiritual beings in a body! Our spirit our soul really is ever present, that love is transportive and transforming and is essential to our life in our human bodies.

A few weeks later, my friend's gramps was very ill in hospital and I had accompanied my friend to the hospital during this time. This particular night we were visiting and the doctor had called my friend aside to tell her there wasn't much more they could do for him. I sat with him as he lay peacefully in front of me drifting in and out of a sleepy state. The I AM I had connected with the week or so before hit me. My perception of life changed, here lay this beautiful soul that up until a few days had been so independent, to lying helpless in a hospital bed. His glasses, shaver, aftershave and watch lay on the bedside table and it struck me how these personal belongings to him became just belongings, that these would continue to be glasses, shaver, aftershave and watch after he passed away.

My other senses had kicked in, I could see the light around him diminishing. What was really powerful was the peace that surrounded him and the love that cocooned my friend and her gramps. There was such a strong love bond between them and it was so beautiful to witness and truly grateful to be allowed to see. Heart-breaking at the same time, as they waited on Mother Nature taking her course and the sense of helplessness. It's in these moments, we realise how precious life is and how much time and energy we waste on getting hung up on material possessions, when in essence the love we have in our hearts and the connections and memories we have made, are all that truly matter.

Understanding I AM puts things in perspective and allows you to appreciate yourself more authentically and the simple things around you. The breath we take for granted becomes so precious. I know I value each breath I take now and treasure the depth each breath takes me allowing me to release all the emotional trauma I no longer need as it serves no purpose to me or anyone else, lightening my load, freeing my body and my mind.

I hope this has provoked questions inside you? If so, pause, write them down and think. The power of writing things down is great, don't under estimate it.

I was urged to write an I AM list, I have done this previously mindlessly and not believing it to be true of me, now I read my list daily and breathe into the I Am that, I am.

I am love, I am

I am full of peace, I am

I am happy, I am

I am successful, I am

I am abundant in all the riches of life, I am

I am beautiful, I am

I am vibrant, I am

I am full of energy, I am

You can add or adapt this list. I have more that are personal to me. If you have a dream job put it down, I am a dancer, I am a scientist……. The beauty of this there is no right and no wrong you just do what YOU feel and nobody can take that from you. Feel the inner child release within as you write your list, make it full of all the qualities, desires you want no matter how ridiculous, the more outrageous the better. Get the real you out from the depths within, out into the consciousness, ready for the universe to deliver. Feel it, love it, embrace it, laugh at it, fill it with all these energies, be these energies.

I AM I

I am the sun, I am the light, I am the love, I am the part of the universe, I am the part of the creation of all that connects us as one…….. I AM I

We are all strands of the universe making us unique, the unique energies of each strand gives the universe diverse qualities it has to offer, making miracles that appear to us happen, when all along its what's was meant to be, love is the highest energy that allows the miracles to happen…

Be unique

Believe

Trust

Love

And go with the universal flow.

We all perceive life to be so difficult. When really it's quite simple when we understand that life, the universe, the Angels and Mother Earth are all there divinely guiding us all the time, from the moment we are born to the second we die.

When we breathe deeply into the depths of our abdomen and exhale though our mouth, we centre ourselves and bring us back to here and now, we can see before us what we need to see. We allow all preconceived notions to disappear, it's trusting in ourselves to listen to what our bodies and environment is telling us.

As our bodies begin to waken up, we begin to remember who we really are and what we are really about. Our innate gifts and healing surface, guiding us through life.

This Little Light of Mine

One of my favourite wee tunes that comes into my head now and again and it lights me up inside and I feel a silly dance come along as well as I sing it, much to the annoyance or embarrassment of my children, mind you they might not even notice.

"This little light of mine, I'm gonna let it shine, this little light of mine I'm gonna let it shine, let it shine, let it shine "

We all have a light that's inside of us. For some it's expansive, others not so much. The best way to describe is like the advert for the Ready Brek man, where there was a glow round him.

I remember the day I really got it! I had been at church

and few of the people who had been there for a number of years had an amazing energy about them and I remember really being in awe of it. When we were singing you could physically see the light shining around them, they were filled up with universal energy that was palpable, the comparison was some who was new to the congregation had a very small light and I sensed they had lost their path and was at the church to help them find direction and find themselves again. I know I've used religion as an example, but it doesn't really matter what you believe in just that you believe in you, believe in the light and love that fills you up.

Has anyone every walked into a room and you just feel the presence of them, like a magnet that you feel drawn to, or just being in their company you feel calm and at peace, as a serenity comes from them. Or we use statements like "she just lit up the room when she arrived".

Our inner lights dim when we have come off our path, we get caught up in day to day stuff and things of the past that makes us sad and we get stuck in the turmoil of emotion it created, we forget us and who we are.

We need to give ourselves the time and the space to be true to our soul.

What makes you light up inside?

What sparks the passion inside you?

For me, it's getting in the flow and writing. Anything

connected to spirituality and health and healing, listening to music that takes me to a different place. Watching my children grow, listening to them and what lights them up inside. Everyone is different, have a think of what makes you light up, you may even be surprised.

Sing, laugh, dance like no one's watching and allow you to be yourself. I have a funny journal of things throughout my life that made me laugh and smile, so at any point when I feel low or need a boost, I can read it and refer back to it, to lift my vibration and make me laugh.

Go on make your laughter memories you be glad you did.

One of my memories was when I was married, and we had visited my ex-husbands dad in the north of Scotland. One Sunday we went to a place called Colbackie beach. I was a beautiful beach with lovely sand dunes. My ex-husband and his dad decided to run up these steep dunes and his dad began to run down at an angle as they were so steep, my ex-husband ran straight down! He wasn't long started his decent and he went head first and ended up rolling all the way down this dune that seemed to never end. It was like a live cartoon, with slow motion. The sand flying up at the back of him, me at the bottom absolutely poor less with laughter, my sides ached so much from this image of him rolling down this dune, at the bottom he was covered in sand from head to toe. I had to be helped up from laughing so much. When we got back and he showered, there was sand in every imaginable place, for weeks he was still finding sand, sometimes I just had to look at him and burst out laughing! I could never get the story out without being in kinks laughing, tears streaming down my face. The image is so ingrained in my brain, even as I write this it makes me laugh so much.

Light and love, fill yourself daily with these two things and life will always work in your favour, even in a dark time there is always light should we wish to see it. Be the ball of love you want to be, to help anyone in life you have to be you, love you. When you understand love, you have the ultimate key to the universe and it all starts with you.

Love and light is our way forward. As each individual regains their self, we collectively can change the world. We are the light workers in motion, some more aware than others, as each one grows we will attract others to our shining light and love, as we hold a space for others to feel the same connection in themselves, as we initiate the spark inside them.

In one of my groups, we discussed this and one commented that there are situations that no amount of love and deep breathing would help. I had to disagree. If you were in the flow you would be in control of your destiny and what lies ahead, however, sad things can happen around us that might rob our energy a little if we allow it. People connected round about us are on a different journey and we need to be careful not to get caught up in their journey and we need to detach emotionally from their situations, doesn't mean we can't listen to them, but remember energetically to give them their "stuff" back with love so they can deal with it and not remain stuck where they are.

I had a client who came for a therapy every week for a few weeks, before each session we would do some deep breathing and centring herself, so when we did the therapy she was able to get more out of it. By doing this, it helped her realise how disconnected from herself she had become. She was caught up in family life and she had been forgotten about. I gave her some tips and sure enough a few weeks passed and you could see the light in her getting brighter. She had reconnected back to herself and ignited the spark within. She was inspired to write/blog about her situations and made her realise that she herself did have a story to tell, that could help others. She noticed things in her family dynamics change for the better, this all happened with her going within, making that change and allowing the love and light in.

What was interesting about her coming to me was there was someone closer to her that offered the same therapy, but she felt drawn to come to me. She didn't know why at first but now she does. She trusted her instincts and the synchronicity between us and the connection through books we had read and were able to share, that she couldn't with others, allowed her to be herself and know that it's ok to do so.

When I help facilitate people to get back on their path, to do their inner work, and see their world change for the better, that lights me up more than anything.

I truly believe everything in life happens for a reason, good and bad. Each day is a brand new day to start again.

Light is shining down on us all the time, it's this light that is awakening our souls within and is taking us back to our innate senses, light is guiding us from the darkness.

Love and Light Mediation

Take a nice long deep breath in………. and let it go, feeling all the tension and stress leave your body.

Take another deep long breath in……. and let it go, feeling all the muscles of the body relax and melt away the tensions.

Take another long deep breath in………. and let it go, feeling relaxed and centred.

Imagine your crown chakra open and a beam of pure brilliant white light pouring in, down through your body.

Feel this light as it filters its way through all the cells and fibres of your being clearing away any darkness and filling it with light.

(Pause for a few minutes)

Feel your being expand as the light fills you, feel your heart chakra as it opens and beams love and light out connecting you to everything and everyone. Feel the oneness of the universe right inside of you, be the light, bask in this light, dance with your angels let them take you on a journey of the light.

(Pause for five minutes or longer)

Feel the I AM that's inside you, feel the peace within you.

(Pause)

As your angles bring you back to your heart chakra where you began your dance of the light, you feel physically lighter, more energised and clearer in mind, body and spirit.

You thank your angels for this wonderful experience.

You begin to return yourself to the room.

Three deep breaths and you are back in the here and now.

Give yourself a few moments to come back, write down

your experience and insight during the meditation.

Angels are everywhere every day and in every way. We spoke earlier in the root chakra about how to recognise angels nearby, by now you should be working with them daily, it's easy to get out the habit, I know when I don't, things don't go as smoothly as they should reminding me how close they are when we need them, but we need to remember to ask.

I love working with my angels, I am always amazed at how they keep me on my path. Knowing that when I am in alignment with them they are working with the universe to bring my dreams into reality, this book being one of them. They have guided me well on my journey and my trust and faith in them grow daily. It's such a privilege to feel guided and protected.

It takes courage to come out of the spiritual closet as they say! Some people think that you're off your head. But the difference is, you know what your experiencing, you know what's happening is more than a coincidence. I would never have believed I could write a book, I trusted the guidance I was given and here I am. I was so sceptical prior to my journey but curious. I am so grateful for my spirituality and my passion for complementary therapies combined together, never in a day do I feel I work!

We always look for the ever so complicated way of doing things, when often the perceived impossible is in front of our noses and so simple, im'possible, now that makes things simpler and possible.

Life is simple when we go back to our roots and listen from within.

We as a society, have created time and stress. These didn't exist before, but as our science and technology have advanced we have disassociated ourselves from the beats of Mother Earth in the process.

Earth is rebelling trying to get our attention to wake up and go back to the way things should be, the way existence and purpose was.

We should be taking time for ourselves.

We should be ourselves.

We should just be, just be in the moment in the now.

The heart is so profoundly important. This is what we are beginning to awaken to. When we work from the heart, speak from the heart, live from the heart, you are in the truest and purest way of life and abundance comes to you in many manners of means. Accept trust and embrace these moments as you have been divinely guided to be at this time. Synchronicity is continually in motion for us, do not doubt this, creating events for us to grow from, spiritually, to trust in the universe and ourselves. From this point, empowerment is strengthened, bonds are created with our angels by our side but also with other close allies that become heart friends and mentors.

A friend recently said that they aspire to be like me which took me aback! Why would anyone want to be like me? I felt it a huge compliment which I gratefully received, but uneasy at the thought of being on a pedestal. The negative chatter about myself did rear its head for a few moments, I am no one special and why would anyone want to be like me? What did dawn on me was the fact she saw my light, I was being me, being true to myself, nothing more nothing less. What she was aspiring to be was herself, to turn her light on and be seen for who she is, but doesn't yet recognise it in herself yet. She will get there as she has me prompting her daily. When we try to be like someone else we lose ourselves in the process not recognising the points that we have to offer that make us unique.

As I was writing this book, I had a few wobbles along the way, doubting myself, who am I, why would anyone want to read my story? Then a series of synchronised events happened that made me realise that I was on my right path. Random conversations with people who I then mentioned I was writing a book were inspired and eager to hear what I had written about and even read! Then at an event in my local town a medium had come up and said "Yes, do it". I was a bit surprised as it was my book that was on my mind at the time, with the ego battling away, so I knew it was the book she was referring to, which encouraged me.

Then the lightbulb ah moment!!! I was watching Dr

Wayne Dyers movie *The Shift*. I hadn't seen it before and it was just after his sad passing. I realised in that moment that my book was important as I was being of service, as we are all of service in many ways as he says it's the only life purpose we have and it put into context everything that I have written, about becoming our authentic self being in the now, nothing else matters. I had been that person in the movie where a woman's list of priorities before the shift looked like family, independence, career.... Then after the shift the priorities change to growth, peace, spirituality, happiness, which I now have.

Seeing the movie at that point in my life, validated everything for me, that I truly had connected to source on so many occasions prior to the "shift" and was now living my life being truly me, trusting in source and that I am attracting all that I am and are.

In reading other books by Dr Wayne Dyer, Rebecca Campbell, David Hamilton and so many others I felt privileged that I too am being channelled the same messages, that source is connecting us all together to make sure the message is getting out and that truths about ourselves are being discovered.

In growing spiritually, we naturally become mediumistic, intuitive, psychic and a healer as these are our divine tools that have been given to us but forgotten along the way. These were all skills I wanted to learn, but in developing them I found me the real me and that's the biggest gift of all.

It's taken years of learning to let go and clearing the rubbish that I held on to, letting go of old beliefs and patterns. The biggest lesson was letting go of judgement. Not that I judged people, I often take people at face value which did at some points in my life lead to my kindness being taken advantage of. The biggest judgements I had to let go of were of myself. People will always have a judgement about you, it's how you deal with it or not. We are all entitled to opinions and that's all life is opinions of each other or things, doesn't make any one opinion more valid than the next.

When we understand the universal language and just being in the now, simplicity and abundance come and flow to us. We free stress from our body and our mind and we feel physically lighter, we find our way.

Life Purpose

Working on ourselves will naturally throw up questions and doubts.

What is my life purpose?

Why am I here?

There has to be more to life?

Why do I feel lost or stuck?

By now, working through the chakras we have unlocked parts of us, life seems different when you work from the heart centre. We question our being. We realise that it's time to follow our dreams and desires rather than doing what we were taught to do. It's time to wake up as we realise we are not all meant to be the same. We are unique in every way, it's in following our heart intentions we can lead a more spiritually fulfilled life.

When I talk to clients and friends, I ask them what they desire to do and what creates a passion inside them. Then I encourage them to do that. It's the journey from the brain to the heart that takes the longest and trusting in the process. It's letting go of the beliefs that were instilled in us and letting our imagination create our future and our desires, after all, everything around us came from someone's imagination.

One friend I have wanted to do midwifery but lacked confidence in applying, well that was until she had me coaching and encouraging her. By getting her to go within and reconnecting to herself, she unlocked the answers that were deep inside, her calling was midwifery. Meditations we done, cards that were pulled symbols she saw, were all encouragement for what her desires were. She kept the feelings going and the universe transpired and aligned with her and she breezed through the process, not without the ego jumping in now and again. When she applied she was one of 600 odd applicants. She then made the 150 for interview and was then selected as one of the 40 odd for the course and is now living her dream. We worked on clearing old beliefs and patterns and building her confidence and self-esteem to be herself, which is all we can be.

Being of service to ourselves and others is what our life purpose entails. That we can achieve, from any walk of life. We are human and lead a human existence which we need to honour and respect, but if every day we are making small changes and letting our ego diminish, we are working in divine guidance creating the abundance in our life, enriching our soul and our essence.

When we break away from the conformity of society, we really embrace who we really are and we are ready to allow our light to shine. When we trust and take that side step, we realise how trapped we have been.

Crystals for the Crown Chakra

- Amethyst
- Ametrine
- Danburite
- Opalite
- Ruby in Zoisite
- Selenite
- Celestite

Essential Oils for the Crown Chakra

- Cedarwood
- Elemi
- Frankincense
- Jasmine
- Lavendar
- Myrrh
- Neroli
- Rose
- Sandalwood
- Vetiver

Message from the Angels

The message that is being shared is that of love and compassion, which we so desperately need at this time on earth more than ever.

Change is happening all around us right now, big changes that will shake up the whole planet everything from governments, humanitarian issues, the way of life, our work, other people's work.

We so desperately need to go back to old ways. Stress has to be lifted from our lives, our advancement in disease control is working against us, we have the knowledge yet disease and chronic illness is high, our earth is screaming at us to change.

Change begins with one person. We need to become one again, not differentiate between race, colour, religion or class we are all equal. Equal in birth, arriving with nothing. Equal in death, departing with nothing. So why compete with material possessions in between?

Discover your light within and see the world around you in a different way.

Soul Star Chakra

This chakra is located 6 inches or so above the crown chakra. This is where your true spiritual enlightenment occurs and instant manifestations happen. Reaching here, you are accepting your life purpose and embracing it. Manifesting no longer becomes something to practice it's a daily integration of life and we attract what we desire. We have more control over our thought processes and life is more positive.

Our life is more in sync with what's meant to be happening, synchronicity is consistently occurring, encouraging you along the way and growth is continually evolving.

Telepathy skills are more honed in than ever before, or

more that you're more aware of the skill you've always had.

I laugh now in my practice, when I have clients in and I'm thinking of my next question to ask, then next thing they are volunteering the information without me having to verbalise it, it's amazing. These things never cease to amaze me and I never tire of it.

More and more of late, I'm am having clients come for one treatment then discovering so much more and the reason they are there is because they are starting a new path of themselves and by talking to me they can be themselves more openly, talking spiritually and about angels and experiences, without being judged by friends and family around them.

Being spiritual doesn't have to be airy fairy. Once you recognise and feel the flow of the universe and the great power of earth and that you can work with, you can change your life. Consciousness of people is growing and evolving and more people are having their lights switched on and stepping on to a new life path.

My biggest lesson was love and understanding it from a different perspective. That love is a great energy that we can tap into and be a channel of love, that we can make positive change around us by focusing on ourselves, it's really that simple. By embracing life, the positive and negative allowing us not to dwell but make positive action.

As you start your journey, keep note or track of all the things you have noticed change in, your life.

What do you see differently?

What can you tolerate less?

Are you aware of more sensitivities with what you eat?

Are you seeing more blessings?

Is synchronicity occurring more frequently?

Do you hear more things?

Do you see things for the future more clearly?

Is the chatter in your head quieter?

The list could go on, but you get the idea.

In the sacral chakra I touched briefly on nutrition, I just want to discuss this a little more here as I feel the more open we become the more sensitive we are to food stuff.

Nutrition – How it affects us

Don't worry this isn't to preach about a new fad diet or anything like that, but just a point to make about what we eat and how it affects our bodies.

We live now where much of the people we know and love

have some sort of condition such as:

- Depression
- IBS
- Constant bloating
- Headaches/migraines
- Muscle ache or joint pain
- Tiredness
- Dry skin
- Nausea
- Constipation

And the list goes on. What is interesting is the amount of people that think that's just normal! That, that's how you're meant to feel as you get older!

With these conditions, there is a common factor in our diets that we can change that can greatly improve how we feel.

So what is this that we eat that makes us feel poorly?

Gluten.

Gluten is a protein that's found in the majority of grains and here in the west, our diets are made up from grains including breads, pasta, cereals, cakes, biscuits, ready meals, stock cubes, beer, and ketchup the list goes on. All our daily foods contain gluten. So it's easy to see how it can build up in our system.

Gluten is a double binded protein that our bodies find hard to digest so our body then has to work harder to break it down. To get an idea, a slice of bread takes 5 days to break down the gluten. So if you're a bread lover and have a few slices of bread a day, pasta and maybe a wee cake or biscuit, it's easy to see in just one day that our body has a months' worth of gluten to cope with. Over time this then builds up and our bodies react to it. For some they will become coeliac and others diabetes or ME or many other chronic conditions.

This shows that you don't have to be coeliac (an allergy to gluten), but you can be sensitive to it. And like everything else can be had in moderation if not coeliac. As our bodies become more aligned we become more sensitive to food and what it does to our bodies, we are more aware of what our bodies need. Gluten, dairy, some meats and sugar, can all become problematic.

Over that last decade or so, conditions such as coeliac, Crohn's, colitis, fibromyalgia, ME, thyroid disorders are all on the increase and we can do something about it by changing our diets.

I've spoken about gluten specifically because of its impact on our health and how it affects our energy and energy is what we become in tune with. There's far more to cover on gluten and its effects but that's for another time.

If you want to boost your energy and feel emotionally better, a gluten free diet really will help. Set yourself a challenge to stick to a gluten free diet for 6 weeks and see how you feel. It brings your body into alignment, eliminating gluten will allow you to be more intuitive with your body.

The *Grain Brain* by Dr David Perlmutter is a good read to find out more about the effects of gluten if you want to read more.

I've been gluten and dairy free now for a few years and feel the amazing benefit of leaving it out my diet. My energy is good and my body is happier. If I have accidentally eaten gluten I really feel the impact, pain in my body, mood can sink and I realise it's not worth eating it to feel so rubbish.

Daily Checklist

Here is a daily checklist which I advise to do throughout the day.

1. Deep breaths mainly in the morning, however as often as you can throughout the day or in times of stress or panic.

2. Meditate, even if it is only for 5 minutes in the day it will make a difference to your day. Longer if you can or at least once a week 30 mins meditation.

3. Write Gratitude journal, daily, list a minimum of five things that's happened during the day that you are grateful for.

4. Dance like no one is watching

Reading list

Wishes Fulfilled - Dr Wayne Dyer

Light is the New Black – Rebecca Campbell

The Lightworkers Way – Doreen Virtue

I Heart Me – David Hamilton

Loveability – Robert Holden

The Daily Love Growing into Grace – Mastin Kipp

The 11.11 Code: Secrets of the Convent – Hilary H Carter

E-Squared – Pam Grout

Dying to Be Me – Anita Moorjani

Conscious Medicine – Gill Edwards

27879801R00107

Printed in Poland
by Amazon Fulfillment
Poland Sp. z o.o., Wrocław